125 best
Vegetarian
Slow Cooker
recipes

125 best Vegetarian Slow Cooker recipes

Judith Finlayson

Robert ROSE

For complete cataloguing information, see page 180.

Disclaimer

Design & Production: PageWave Graphics Inc.
Editor: Carol Sherman
Recipe Testers: Jennifer MacKenzie and Audrey King
Copy Editor: Julia Armstrong
Photography: Mark T. Shapiro
Food Styling: Kate Bush
Prop Styling: Charlene Erricson

Cover image: Succulent Succotash (see recipe, page 115)

The publisher and author wish to express their appreciation to the following suppliers of props used in the food photography:

DISHES, LINENS, ACCESSORIES

Homefront
371 Eglinton Avenue West
Toronto, Ontario M5N 1A3
Tel: (416) 488-3189
www.homefrontshop.com

The Kitchen and Glass Place
804 Yonge Street
Toronto, Ontario, M4W 2H1
Tel: (416) 927-9925

Pier 1 Imports
Toronto, Ontario

FLATWARE
Gourmet Settings Inc.
245 West Beaver Creek Road, Unit 10
Richmond Hill, Ontario L4B 1L1
Tel: 1-800-551-2649
www.gourmetsettings.com

We acknowledge the financial support of the Government of Canada through the Book Publishing Industry Development Program (BPIDP) for our publishing activities.

Published by Robert Rose Inc.
120 Eglinton Avenue East, Suite 800, Toronto, Ontario, Canada M4P 1E2
Tel: (416) 322-6552 Fax: (416) 322-6936

Printed in Canada

6 7 8 9 10 11 12 CPL 14 13 12 11 10 09 08

In memory of Catherine Dees

Acknowledgments

Once again, my thanks to the great creative team who work behind the scenes to ensure that my books achieve the highest degree of excellence in editing, photography, styling and design. All the folks at PageWave Graphics, Andrew Smith, Joseph Gisini, Kevin Cockburn and Daniella Zanchetta, for their great design work; my editor Carol Sherman, who is always on top of my shortcomings, yet consistently tactful and fun to work with; Kate Bush and Charlene Erricson for their talented styling; and last, but certainly not least, Mark Shapiro for his beautiful photographs, which make all my recipes look delicious.

Special thanks to Jennifer MacKenzie and Audrey King for their diligent help with recipe testing and to all my family, friends and neighbors, who gallantly tuck in to my culinary creations, even those that miss the mark, and provide thoughtful comments that are always useful in fine-tuning the end result.

I'd also like to thank Jennifer Grange at The Cookbook Store for pointing me in the direction of this topic and Bob Dees and Marian Jarkovich at Robert Rose for their consistent commitment to ensuring that my books are well received in the marketplace.

Contents

Introduction

Since writing my first slow cooker book, I've become even more convinced of the value of this amazing appliance. Not only is it a great convenience, it fits so well with the way I like to cook that it constantly inspires me to think of new ways to incorporate its services into my life. Given our increased emphasis on nutrition, the time seemed right to do a book focused exclusively on vegetarian recipes. Today, many people — even those who are not vegetarians — are eating less meat. Not only is a diet high in vegetables, legumes, grains and fruit lower in calories and saturated fat, plant foods have many other health benefits, such as disease-fighting properties, which we are only now beginning to understand. Combining the advantages of eating more vegetables with the convenience of the slow cooker seemed like a great idea.

As in my previous books, I've tried to include a wide range of recipes that will appeal to many tastes and requirements — from great family food to more sophisticated recipes for entertaining, including desserts. There are more than 60 "vegan-friendly" recipes in the book, which have been identified as such for easy access. And many recipes that contain eggs or dairy can be easily substituted with egg substitutes and/or non-diary ingredients that suit your taste.

As a committed slow cooker fan, it doesn't surprise me that the slow cooker, invented in the 1970s as a device for cooking beans, is enjoying a lively revival in the early years of the new millennium. Quite simply, it is one of the most effective time-management tools any cook can have. With its help, even the most time-pressed people can arrive home after a busy day to an old-fashioned home-cooked meal, ready to serve.

As enjoyable as it is to recreate many of the more traditional dishes that were a meaningful part of the past, such as Blue Plate Chili or Rigatoni and Cheese, in developing this book I've also had great fun experimenting with more exotic dishes that reflect the expanding horizons of home cooking in our global world. Creamy Braised Fennel, with an intriguing sauce flavored with lemon and saffron and Parsnip and Coconut Curry with Crispy Shallots are two favorites that represent Mediterranean and South-East Asian cultures, respectively. I particularly enjoy using herbs and spices in such dishes as Caribbean Pepper Pot Soup, Black Bean Torta and Vegetable Curry with Pepper and Cilantro Tadka. And I love updating old standards such as French Onion Soup or transforming dishes such as Stroganoff into a vegetarian version.

There's more to using a slow cooker than putting food on the table. In my opinion, the meals it allows you to prepare nourish both body and soul. Made from fresh and wholesome ingredients, with levels of fat and salt controlled by the home cook, slow cooker dishes are certainly nutritious. But more than that, they offer a reassuring antidote to the stresses of our fast-paced, high-tech age. There are few experiences more pleasurable than arriving home to be greeted by the appetizing aroma of a simmering soup or stew, the kinds of dishes that the slow cooker excels at producing.

About six million slow cookers are sold every year. This makes it one of our most popular appliances, which isn't surprising since it is also one of the easiest to use. Once the food is in the slow cooker, you can usually forget about it until it's ready to serve. With the slow cooker's help, anyone can prepare delicious food with a minimum of attention and maximum certainty of success. I sincerely hope you will try these recipes and that you will enjoy them and make the slow cooker a regular part of your life.

— *Judith Finlayson*

Using Your Slow Cooker

An Effective Time Manager

In addition to producing great-tasting food, a slow cooker is one of the most effective time-management tools available. Once the ingredients have been prepared and assembled in the stoneware and the appliance is turned on, you can pretty much forget about it. The slow cooker performs unattended while you carry on with your workaday life. You can be away from the kitchen all day and return to a hot, delicious meal.

A Low-Tech Appliance

Slow cookers are amazingly low tech. The appliance usually consists of a metal casing and a stoneware insert with a tight-fitting lid. For convenience, this insert should be removable from the metal casing, making it easier to clean and increasing its versatility as a serving dish. The casing contains the heat source: electrical coils. These coils do their work using the energy it takes to power a 100-watt light bulb. Because the slow cooker operates on such a small amount of energy, you can safely leave it turned on while you are away from home.

Slow Cooker Basics

Slow cookers are generally round or oval and range in size from 1 to 7 quarts. The small round ones are ideal for dips and fondues, as well as some soups, main courses and desserts. The larger sizes, usually oval, are necessary to cook recipes, such as savory custards and some desserts that need to be prepared in a dish or pan, which fits into the stoneware.

Because I use my slow cookers a lot for entertaining, I feel there is a benefit to having two: a smaller (3 to 4 quart) one, which is ideal for preparing dips, roasting nuts or making recipes with smaller yields; and a larger (6 quart) oval one, which is necessary for cooking large quantities of stew-like dishes, as well as for making recipes that call for setting a baking dish or pan inside the stoneware. Once you begin using your slow cooker, you will get a sense of what your own needs are.

Some manufacturers sell a "slow cooker" that is actually a multi-cooker. It has a heating element at the bottom and, in my experience, it cooks faster than a traditional slow cooker. Also, since the heat source is at the bottom, it is possible that the food will scorch during the long cooking time unless it is stirred.

Your slow cooker should come with a booklet that explains how to use the appliance. I recommend that you read this carefully and/or visit the manufacturer's web site for specific information on the model you purchased. I've cooked with a variety of slow cookers and have found that cooking times can vary substantially from one to another. Although it may not seem particularly helpful if you're just starting out, the only firm advice I can give is: Know your slow cooker. After trying a few of these recipes, you will get a sense of whether your slow cooker is faster or slower than the ones I use, and you will be able to adjust the cooking times accordingly.

Other variables that can affect cooking time are extreme humidity, power fluctuations and high altitudes. Be extra vigilant if any of these circumstances affects you.

Cooking Great-Tasting Food

The slow cooker's less-is-better approach is, in many ways, the secret of its success. The appliance does its work by cooking foods very slowly — from about 200°F (90°C) on the Low setting to 300°F (150°C) on High. This slow, moist cooking environment (remember the tight-fitting lid) enables the appliance to produce mouth-watering braises, chilies and many other kinds of soups and stews. It also helps to ensure success with delicate puddings and custards, among other dishes.

Some Benefits of Long, Slow Cooking

- Allows the seasoning in complex sauces to mingle without scorching.
- Makes succulent chilies and stews that don't dry out or stick to the bottom of the pot.
- The low, even heat helps to ensure success with delicate dishes such as puddings and custards.

Slow Cooker Tips

Understanding Your Slow Cooker

Like all appliances, the slow cooker has its unique way of doing things and, as a result, you need to understand how it works and adapt your cooking style accordingly. When friends learned I was writing a slow cooker cookbook, many had a similar response: "Oh, you mean that appliance that allows you to throw the ingredients in and return to a home-cooked meal!"

"Well, sort of," was my response. Over the years, I've learned to think of my slow cooker as an indispensable helpmate and I can hardly imagine living without its assistance. But I also know that it can't work miracles. Off the top of my head, I can't think of any great dish that results when ingredients are merely "thrown together." Success in the slow cooker, like success in the oven or on top of the stove, depends upon using proper cooking techniques. The slow cooker saves you time because it allows you to forget about the food once it is in the stoneware. But you still must pay attention to the advance preparation. Here are a few tips that will help to ensure slow cooker success.

Soften Vegetables

Although it requires using an extra pan, I am committed to softening most vegetables before adding them to the slow cooker. In my experience, this is not the most time-consuming part of preparing a slow cooker dish — it usually takes longer to peel and chop the vegetables, which you have to do anyway. But softening vegetables such as onions and carrots, dramatically improves the quality of the dish for two reasons: not only does it add color, it begins the process of caramelization, which breaks down their natural sugars and releases the flavor; it also extracts the fat-soluble components of foods, which further enriches the taste. Moreover, tossing herbs and spices with the softened vegetables emulsifies their flavor, helping to produce a sauce in which the flavors are better integrated into the dish than they would have been if this step had been skipped.

Reduce Liquid

As you use your slow cooker, one of the first things you will notice is that it generates a tremendous amount of liquid. Because slow cookers cook at a low heat, tightly covered, liquid doesn't evaporate as it does in the oven or on top of the stove. As a result, food made from traditional recipes will be watery. So the second rule of successful slow cooking is to reduce the amount of liquid. Naturally, you don't want to reduce the flavor, so I suggest using vegetable stock, rather than water, to cook most of the dishes. The other potential problem with liquid generation is that it can affect the results of starch dishes, such as cakes and some grains. One technique, which works well with such dishes, is to place folded tea towels over top of the stoneware before covering with the lid. This prevents accumulated moisture from dripping on the food.

Cut Root Vegetables into Thin Slices or Small Pieces

Perhaps surprisingly, root vegetables — carrots, parsnips, turnips and, particularly, potatoes — cook very slowly in the slow cooker. As a result, root vegetables should be thinly sliced or cut into small pieces no larger than 1-inch (2.5 cm) cubes.

Pay Attention to Cooking Temperature

Many desserts, such as those containing milk, cream or some leavening agents, need to be cooked on High. In these recipes, a Low setting is not suggested as an option. For recipes that aren't dependent upon cooking at a particular temperature, the rule of thumb is that 1 hour of cooking on High equals 2 to $2\frac{1}{2}$ hours on Low.

Don't Overcook

Although slow cooking reduces your chances of overcooking food, it is still not a "one size fits all" solution to meal preparation. Many vegetables such as beans, lentils and root vegetables need a good 8 hour cooking span and may even benefit from a longer cooking time. But others, such as green beans and cauliflower, are usually cooked within 6 hours on Low and will be overcooked and unappetizing if left for longer. One solution (which is not possible if you are cooking meat because of food safety concerns) is to extend the cooking time by assembling the dish ahead, then refrigerating it overnight in the stoneware. Because the mixture and the stoneware are chilled, the vegetables will take longer to cook. This is a useful technique if you are cooking more tender vegetables and need to be away from the house all day.

Use Ingredients Appropriately

Some ingredients do not respond well to long, slow cooking at all, and should be added during the last 30 minutes of cooking, after the temperature has been increased to High. These include zucchini, peas, snow peas, milk and cream (which will curdle if cooked too long).

Since I am not a vegan, many of my recipes contain dairy products. I have not suggested non-dairy alternatives because in my experience, the flavor and manufacturing standards vary dramatically among products and brands, affecting recipe results. If you do not eat dairy, I assume you will be well aware of the alternatives and will have sourced the products that work for you. Try a few of the recipes using non-diary alternatives, for example olive oil for butter, egg replacement products for eggs, soft tofu or soy yogurt for yogurt, cashew or soy milk for milk or cream, the many varieties of soy cheese for those made from milk and ices or soy ice cream for whipped or ice cream. You will soon get a feel for those that produce satisfactory results.

Although I love to cook with peppers, I've learned that most peppers become bitter if cooked for too long. The same holds true for cayenne pepper or hot pepper sauces such as Tabasco, and large quantities of spicy curry powder. (Small quantities of mild curry powder seem to fare well, possibly because natural sugars in the vegetables counter any bitterness.) The solution to this problem is to add fresh green or red bell peppers to recipes during the last 30 minutes of cooking, use cayenne pepper in small quantities, if at all, and add hot pepper sauce after the dish is cooked. I have also found that several varieties of dried peppers, such as New Mexico or ancho chilies, which become bitter if added to the slow cooker when dry or not fully rehydrated, work well if they are thoroughly soaked in boiling water for 30 minutes before being added to slow cooker recipes. All the recipes in this book address these concerns in the instructions.

Whole Leaf Herbs and Spices

For best results, use whole or coarsely ground, rather than finely ground, herbs and spices in the slow cooker. Whole or coarsely ground spices, such as cumin seeds, and whole leaf herbs, such as dried thyme and oregano leaves, release their flavors slowly throughout the long cooking period, unlike finely ground spices and herbs, which tend to lose flavor during slow cooking. If you're using fresh herbs, add them finely chopped during the last hour of cooking unless you include the whole stem (this works best with thyme and rosemary).

I recommend the use of cracked black peppercorns rather than ground pepper in many of my recipes because they release flavor slowly during the long cooking process. "Cracked pepper" can be purchased in the spice sections of supermarkets, but I like to make my own in a mortar with a pestle. If you prefer to use ground black pepper, use one-quarter to half the amount of cracked black peppercorns called for in the recipe.

Using Dishes and Pans in the Slow Cooker

Some recipes, notably puddings and custards, need to be cooked in an extra dish placed in the slow cooker stoneware. Not only will you need a large oval slow cooker for this purpose, finding a dish or pan that fits into the stoneware can be a challenge. I've found that standard 7-inch (17.5 cm) square, 4-cup (1 L) and 6-cup (1.5 L) ovenproof baking dishes are the best all-round dishes for this purpose, and I've used them to cook most of the custard-like recipes in this book. A 7-inch (17.5 cm) springform pan, which fits into a large oval slow cooker, is also a useful purchase for making cheesecakes and other desserts.

Before you decide to make a recipe requiring a baking dish, ensure that you have a container that will fit into your stoneware. I've noted the size and dimensions of the containers used in all relevant recipes. Be aware that varying the size and shape of the dish is likely to affect cooking times.

Maximize Slow Cooker Convenience

Although slow cookers can produce mouth-watering food, the appliance's other great strength is convenience. Where appropriate, all my recipes contain a make-ahead tip to help you maximize this attribute. To get the most out of your slow cooker, consider the following:

- Prepare ingredients to the cooking stage the night before you intend to cook, to keep work to a minimum in the morning.
- Cook a recipe overnight and refrigerate until ready to serve.

Starters, Fondues and Savories

Sumptuous Spinach and Artichoke Dip

SERVES 6 TO 8

• • • • •

Although spinach and artichoke dip has become a North American classic, its roots lie in Provençal cuisine, where the vegetables are usually baked with cheese and served as a gratin. This chunky dip, simplicity itself, always draws rave reviews and disappears to the last drop.

• • • • •

Tip

If you prefer a smoother dip, place spinach and artichokes in a food processor, in separate batches, and pulse until desired degree of fineness is achieved. Then combine with remaining ingredients in slow cooker stoneware.

• Works best in a small (maximum 3½ quart) slow cooker

1 cup	shredded mozzarella cheese	250 mL
8 oz	cream cheese, cubed	250 g
¼ cup	freshly grated Parmesan cheese	50 mL
1	clove garlic, minced	1
¼ tsp	freshly ground black pepper	1 mL
1	tin (14 oz/398 mL) artichokes, drained and finely chopped	1
8 oz	fresh spinach leaves or 1 package (10 oz/300 g) spinach, stems removed, washed and finely chopped	250 g
	Tostadas or tortilla chips	

1. In slow cooker stoneware, combine mozzarella, cream cheese, Parmesan, garlic, black pepper, artichokes and spinach. Cover and cook on **High** for 2 hours, until hot and bubbling. Stir well and serve with tostadas or other tortilla chips.

Spicy Spinach Dip

SERVES 6

* * * * *

Here's a great dip with a bit of punch. If you are a heat seeker, add the extra jalapeño pepper and use extra hot salsa.

* * * * *

Tip

If you are using frozen spinach in this recipe, thaw and squeeze the excess moisture out before adding to the slow cooker. If you are using fresh spinach leaves, wash thoroughly in lukewarm water to remove all grit. Dry thoroughly before adding to the slow cooker. If excess moisture is not removed from the dip it will be quite runny — but still delicious!

• Works best in a small (maximum 3½ quart) slow cooker

8 oz	fresh spinach leaves or 1 package (10 oz/300 g) frozen, thawed spinach (see Tip, left)	250 g
2 cups	shredded Monterey Jack cheese	500 mL
½ cup	tomato salsa	125 mL
¼ cup	sour cream	50 mL
4	green onions, white part only, finely chopped	4
1 to 2	jalapeño peppers, seeds removed and finely chopped	1 to 2
¼ tsp	freshly ground black pepper	1 mL
	Tostadas or tortilla chips	

1. In slow cooker stoneware, combine spinach, cheese, salsa, sour cream, green onions, jalapeño peppers and black pepper. Cover and cook on **High** for 2 hours, until hot and bubbling. Stir well and serve with tostadas or other tortilla chips.

Artichoke, Sun-Dried Tomato and Goat Cheese Spread

SERVES 6

• • • • • •

Serve this sophisticated spread on leaves of Belgian endive, topped with toasted pine nuts for added flair. Or spoon it into a pottery bowl and surround with pieces of flat bread for a more informal presentation.

• • • • • •

Tip

To toast pine nuts, place them in a dry skillet, over medium heat. Cook, stirring constantly until they begin to turn a light golden, 3 to 4 minutes. Remove from heat and immediately transfer to a small bowl. Once they begin to brown, they can burn very quickly.

• Works best in a small (maximum 3½ quart) slow cooker

1	can (14 oz/398 mL) artichokes, drained and finely chopped	1
4	sun-dried tomatoes, packed in olive oil, drained and finely chopped	4
2	cloves garlic, crushed	2
¼ tsp	salt	1 mL
¼ tsp	freshly ground black pepper	1 mL
8 oz	soft goat cheese, crumbled	250 g
	Belgian endive (optional)	
¼ cup	toasted pine nuts (optional)	50 mL

1. In slow cooker stoneware, combine artichokes, sun-dried tomatoes, garlic, salt and pepper. Cover and cook on **High** for 1 hour.

2. Add goat cheese and stir to combine. Cover and cook on **High** for 1 hour until hot and bubbling. Stir well. Spoon into a bowl or spread on leaves of Belgian endive and top with toasted pine nuts, if using.

Chilly Dilly Eggplant

SERVES 8 TO 10

• • • • •

This is a versatile recipe, delicious as a dip with raw vegetables or on pita triangles, as well as a sandwich spread on crusty French bread. It also makes a wonderful addition to a mezes or tapas–style meal. Although it is tasty warm, the flavor dramatically improves if it is thoroughly chilled before serving.

• • • • •

Tip

To reduce any bitterness, peel eggplant before using. Sprinkling with salt and leaving the pieces to "sweat" for an hour also draws out the bitter juice. If time is short, blanch the pieces for a minute or two in heavily salted water. In either case, rinse thoroughly in fresh cold water and, using your hands, squeeze out the excess moisture. Pat dry with paper towels and it's ready to cook.

• • • • •

Make ahead

You'll achieve maximum results if you make this a day ahead and chill thoroughly before serving, or cook overnight, purée in the morning and chill.

• Works best in a small (maximum 3½ quart) slow cooker

2	large eggplants, peeled, cut into 1-inch (2.5 cm) cubes and drained of excess moisture (see Tip, left)	2
2 to 3 tbsp	olive oil	25 to 45 mL
2	medium onions, chopped	2
4	cloves garlic, chopped	4
1 tsp	dried oregano leaves	5 mL
1 tsp	salt	5 mL
½ tsp	freshly ground black pepper	2 mL
1 tbsp	balsamic or red wine vinegar	15 mL
½ cup	chopped fresh dill	125 mL
	Dill sprigs (optional)	
	Finely chopped black olives (optional)	

1. In a skillet, heat 2 tbsp (25 mL) oil over medium-high heat. Add eggplant, in batches, and brown. Transfer to slow cooker stoneware.

2. In same pan, using more oil, if necessary, cook onions on medium heat, stirring, until softened, about 3 minutes. Add garlic, oregano, salt and pepper and cook for 1 minute. Transfer to slow cooker and stir to combine thoroughly. Cover and cook on **Low** for 7 to 8 hours or on **High** for 4 hours, until vegetables are tender.

3. Transfer contents of slow cooker (in batches, if necessary) to a blender or food processor work bowl. Add vinegar and dill and process until smooth, scraping down sides of bowl at halfway point. Taste for seasoning and adjust. Spoon into a small serving bowl and chill thoroughly. Garnish with sprigs of dill and chopped black olives, if using.

Hot Roasted Nuts

SERVES 6 TO 8

- - - - -

When entertaining in winter, I like to light a fire and place small bowls full of these tasty nibblers around the living room. I recommend using a small slow cooker for these recipes, as the nuts are less likely to burn. If you use a large slow cooker (5 or 6 quarts), watch carefully and stir every 15 minutes, as the nuts will cook quite quickly (just over an hour).

Everyone loves these hot buttery peanuts — even me, and I'm usually not a fan of this Southern legume. Use peanuts with skins on or buy them peeled, depending upon your preference. Both work well in this recipe.

- These recipes work best in a small (maximum 3½ quart) slow cooker

Salty Almonds with Thyme

2 cups	unblanched almonds	500 mL
½ tsp	white pepper	2 mL
1 tbsp	fine sea salt, or more to taste	15 mL
2 tbsp	extra-virgin olive oil	25 mL
2 tbsp	fresh thyme leaves	25 mL

1. In slow cooker stoneware, combine almonds and white pepper. Cover and cook on **High** for 1½ hours, stirring every 30 minutes, until nuts are nicely toasted.

2. In a mixing bowl, combine salt, olive oil and thyme. Add to hot almonds in stoneware and stir thoroughly to combine. Spoon mixture into a small serving bowl and serve hot or allow to cool.

Buttery Peanuts

2 cups	raw peanuts	500 mL
¼ cup	melted butter or butter substitute	50 mL
2 tsp	fine sea salt	10 mL

1. In slow cooker stoneware, combine peanuts and butter. Cover and cook on **High** for 2 to 2½ hours, stirring occasionally, until peanuts are nicely roasted. Drain on paper towels. Place in a bowl, sprinkle with salt and stir to combine.

Variation

Curried Buttery Peanuts
In a small bowl, combine sea salt with 2 tsp (10 mL) curry powder and a pinch of cayenne pepper. Substitute for plain salt.

If you like nuts with a sweet finish, try these delicious pecans. Don't expect leftovers, as they are very popular.

• • • • •

Tip

Sea salt is available in most supermarkets. It is much sweeter than table salt and is essential for these recipes as table salt would impart an unpleasant acrid taste to the nuts.

Only slightly nippy, with just a hint of cinnamon, these cashews are a tasty and nutritious treat any time of the year.

Orange-Spiced Pecans

2 cups	pecan halves	500 mL
2 tbsp	orange juice	25 mL
¼ cup	granulated sugar	50 mL
I tbsp	grated orange zest	15 mL
½ tsp	ground cinnamon	2 mL
¼ tsp	freshly grated nutmeg	I mL
Pinch	fine sea salt	Pinch

1. In slow cooker stoneware, combine pecans and orange juice. Cover and cook on **High** for 1 hour or until nuts release their aroma and are nicely toasted. Transfer to a serving bowl.

2. In a small bowl, combine sugar, orange zest, cinnamon, nutmeg and salt. Pour over hot nuts and toss to combine. Serve warm.

Spicy Cashews

2 cups	raw cashews	500 mL
I tsp	chili powder	5 mL
½ tsp	cayenne pepper	2 mL
¼ tsp	ground cinnamon	I mL
2 tsp	fine sea salt	10 mL
I tbsp	extra virgin olive oil	15 mL

1. In slow cooker stoneware, combine cashews, chili powder, cayenne and cinnamon. Stir to combine thoroughly. Cover and cook on **High** for 1½ hours, stirring every 30 minutes, until nuts are nicely toasted.

2. In a small bowl, combine sea salt and olive oil. Add to nuts in slow cooker and stir to thoroughly combine. Transfer mixture to a serving bowl. Serve hot or cool.

Variation

Sweet and Spicy Cashews
Substitute 1 tbsp (15 mL) butter for the olive oil and add along with 2 tbsp (25 mL) brown sugar.

Mushroom and Roasted Garlic Crostini

MAKES ENOUGH FOR 28 CROSTINI

• • • • •

Everyone loves this tasty all-purpose hors d'oeuvre, which is both simple and elegant. It can be used as the first course to a dinner or as a party canapé.

• • • • •

Tips

An easy way to roast this quantity of garlic is to peel the cloves, remove the pith (the center part that often sprouts), then place the cloves on a piece of foil. Drizzle about $\frac{1}{2}$ tsp (2 mL) olive oil over the garlic, then fold up the foil to make a tight packet. Bake in 400°F (200°C) oven for 20 minutes.

Leave small mushrooms whole. Cut larger ones into halves or quarters.

Keep a bottle of dry white vermouth on hand as it makes a satisfactory substitute for dry white wine. That way, you don't have to open a bottle of wine when you need only a small quantity.

Cover and refrigerate the mushroom cooking liquid. It is a great addition to soups, stews and gravies, along with or instead of broth.

• Works best in a small (maximum 3 $\frac{1}{2}$ quart) slow cooker

8	cloves roasted garlic (see Tips, left)	8
1 lb	white mushrooms, cleaned and trimmed (see Tips, left)	500 g
2	large French shallots, finely chopped	2
2 tbsp	extra-virgin olive oil	25 mL
$\frac{1}{4}$ cup	dry white wine or dry white vermouth	50 mL
2 tbsp	chopped fresh parsley leaves	25 mL
2 tbsp	whipping (35%) cream (optional)	25 mL
2 tsp	balsamic vinegar	10 mL
	Salt and freshly ground black pepper	
28	crostini (see Tips, page 27)	28
	Crumbled soft goat cheese	

1. In slow cooker stoneware, combine garlic, mushrooms, shallots, olive oil and wine. Cover and cook on **Low** for 8 hours or on **High** for 4 hours, until mushrooms are soft. Drain off liquid (see Tips, left).

2. Place mushroom mixture in a food processor with parsley and pulse until ingredients are very finely chopped but not puréed. Add whipping cream, if using, vinegar, salt and black pepper to taste and pulse two or three times to combine.

3. Preheat oven to 375°F (190°C). Spread mushroom mixture over crostini. Sprinkle goat cheese on top. Place on baking sheet and bake until cheese begins to brown and melt. Serve hot.

Caramelized Onion Crostini

MAKES ABOUT 16 CROSTINI

· · · · ·

Surprise your guests and serve this unusual combination as an *hors d'oeuvre* at your next dinner party. They'll never guess that you haven't been standing over the stove, patiently stirring the onions and coaxing them to caramelize for this delicious treat.

· · · · ·

Tips

If you prefer, season with freshly ground black pepper, to taste, after the onions have finished cooking.

If you don't have fresh thyme, use 2 tbsp (25 mL) finely chopped parsley, instead.

To make crostini: Preheat broiler. Brush baguette slices on both sides with olive oil and toast under broiler, turning once.

3 lbs	onions, peeled and thinly sliced on the vertical (about 6 medium onions)	1.5 kg
3 tbsp	melted butter	45 mL
1 tbsp	granulated sugar	15 mL
1 tsp	salt	5 mL
1 tsp	cracked black peppercorns (see Tips, left)	5 mL
1 tbsp	fresh thyme leaves (see Tips, left)	15 mL
1 tsp	balsamic vinegar	5 mL
16	crostini (see Tips, left)	16
2 cups	shredded Swiss or Gruyère cheese	500 mL

1. In slow cooker stoneware, combine onions and butter. Stir well to coat onions thoroughly. Cover and cook on **High** for 30 minutes to 1 hour, until onions are softened.

2. Add sugar, salt and peppercorns and stir well. Place two clean tea towels, each folded in half (so you will have four layers) over top of stoneware, to absorb the moisture. Cover and cook on **High** for 4 hours, stirring two or three times to ensure that the onions are browning evenly, replacing towels each time. Turn off slow cooker. Stir in thyme and balsamic vinegar.

3. Preheat broiler. Spread onions evenly over crostini and sprinkle cheese evenly over top. Place on baking sheet and broil until cheese is melted and brown, 2 to 3 minutes. Serve immediately.

Chili con Queso

MAKES ABOUT 4 CUPS (1 L)

· · · · · ·

This delicious combination of hot peppers, tomatoes, corn and melted cheese includes versatility as part of its charm. Team it up with tortilla chips or crudités for a great dip. For a light lunch, spread on a warm tortilla, roll up and garnish with chopped green or red onions and sour cream.

· · · · · ·

Tip

If you don't have time to roast a pepper, use good-quality bottled roasted peppers, instead.

• Works best in a small (maximum 3½ quart) slow cooker

I tbsp	vegetable oil	15 mL
2	onions, finely chopped	2
4	cloves garlic, minced	4
I to 2	jalapeño peppers, minced	I to 2
2 tsp	chili powder	10 mL
I tsp	dried oregano leaves	5 mL
I tsp	cracked black peppercorns	5 mL
I tsp	salt	5 mL
2	tomatoes, peeled and diced	2
I cup	corn kernels, thawed if frozen	250 mL
2 cups	shredded Monterey Jack or Cheddar cheese	500 mL
¼ cup	sour cream	50 mL
I	roasted red bell pepper, chopped (optional) (see Tips, page 29)	I

1. In a skillet, heat oil over medium heat. Add onions and cook, stirring, until softened, about 3 minutes. Add garlic, jalapeño pepper, chili powder, oregano, peppercorns and salt and cook, stirring, for 1 minute. Stir in tomatoes and corn and cook until mixture is bubbling. Transfer to slow cooker stoneware.

2. Add cheese, sour cream and red pepper, if using. Stir well. Cover and cook on **High** for 1½ hours, until hot and bubbling.

Black Bean and Salsa Dip

MAKES ABOUT 3 CUPS (750 ML)

• • • • •

This tasty Cuban-inspired dip, which can be made from ingredients you're likely to have on hand, is nutritious and flavorful.

• • • • •

Tips

For a smoother dip, purée the beans in a food processor or mash with a potato masher before adding to stoneware.

If you use a five-alarm salsa in this dip, you may want to omit the jalapeño pepper.

If you don't have time to roast your own pepper, use a bottled roasted red pepper.

To roast peppers: Preheat oven to 400°F (200°C). Place pepper(s) on a baking sheet and roast, turning two or three times, until the skin on all sides is blackened. (This will take about 25 minutes.) Transfer pepper(s) to a heatproof bowl. Cover with a plate and let stand until cool. Remove and, using a sharp knife, lift off skins. Discard skins and slice according to recipe instructions.

• Works best in a small (maximum 3½ quart) slow cooker

1	can (14 to 19 oz/398 to 540 mL) black beans, drained and rinsed or 1 cup (250 mL) dried black beans, cooked and drained (see Basic Beans, page 100)	1
8 oz	cream cheese, cubed	250 g
½ cup	tomato salsa	125 mL
¼ cup	sour cream	50 mL
1 tsp	chili powder	5 mL
1 tsp	cumin seeds (see Tips, page 50)	5 mL
1 tsp	cracked black peppercorns	5 mL
1	jalapeño pepper, finely chopped (optional) (see Tips, left)	1
1	roasted red bell pepper, finely chopped (optional) (see Tips, left)	1
	Finely chopped green onion (optional)	
	Finely chopped cilantro (optional)	

1. In slow cooker stoneware, combine beans, cream cheese, salsa, sour cream, chili powder, cumin seeds, peppercorns, jalapeño pepper and bell pepper, if using. Cover and cook on **High** for 1 hour. Stir again and cook on **High** for an additional 30 minutes, until mixture is hot and bubbling.

2. Serve immediately or set temperature at **Low** until ready to serve. Garnish with green onion and/or cilantro, if desired.

Nippy Cheddar Rabbit

SERVES 6

• • • • •

When I was growing up, my mother's Welsh rarebit was one of my favorite treats. Now that I'm a mother myself, I still think it's yummy, and so does my family. Made with beer, this slightly adult version is a great predinner nibbler for guests. It also doubles as a light luncheon dish served, like mom's, over hot toast.

• Works best in a small (maximum 3½ quart) slow cooker
• Fondue forks

8 oz	old Cheddar cheese, shredded	250 g
I cup	beer	250 mL
2	egg yolks, beaten	2
¼ tsp	dry mustard	I mL
I tbsp	tomato-based chili sauce	I5 mL
I tsp	packed brown sugar	5 mL
Pinch	cayenne pepper	Pinch
	White bread, crusts removed, cut into 1-inch (2.5 cm) cubes and lightly toasted under broiler	

1. In slow cooker stoneware, combine cheese and beer. Cover and cook on **High** for 30 minutes or until cheese melts.

2. In a bowl, whisk together eggs, mustard, chili sauce, brown sugar and cayenne. Pour mixture into slow cooker stoneware and stir until thickened.

3. Spear toasted bread with fondue forks and dip in cheese, ensuring that guests have napkins or plates to catch any dripping sauce.

Creamy Italian Fondue

SERVES 6 TO 8

• • • • •

Although Swiss Fondue has become the standard against which others are measured, other countries have their own techniques for making delicious dips with hot melted cheese. One of my favorites is Fonduta, a particularly rich and creamy fondue that comes from the Piedmontese region of Italy. I like to serve this with chunks of focaccia, a crusty Italian bread, but any crusty white bread will do. Since the sauce is runny — part of its unctuous charm — pass napkins or small plates to catch drips. You can also serve this as a sauce over slices of grilled polenta, which turns it into a plated appetizer eaten with forks.

• • • • •

Tip

Because this fondue doesn't cook for a long time, I prefer to put the garlic through a press rather than mincing to ensure that the flavor is fully integrated into the cheese mixture. If you don't have a garlic press, a fine mince will do.

• Works best in a small (maximum 3½ quart) slow cooker
• Fondue forks

3 cups	shredded Fontina cheese	750 mL
¾ cup	half-and-half (10%) cream	175 mL
1 tbsp	unsalted butter, melted	15 mL
½	small clove garlic, put through a press (see Tip, left)	½
2	egg yolks	2
2 tbsp	hot milk	25 mL
¼ tsp	freshly ground black pepper	1 mL
	Chunks of crusty bread	

1. In slow cooker stoneware, combine cheese and cream. Cover and cook on **Low** for 1 hour. Increase heat to **High**.

2. In a small bowl, combine melted butter and garlic. Pour mixture into cheese mixture, stirring well, until thoroughly combined and the cheese is completely melted.

3. In a bowl, beat egg yolks with hot milk. Add to cheese mixture, stirring to thoroughly combine. Add pepper and stir.

4. Spear bread with fondue forks and dip in sauce, ensuring that guests have napkins or plates to catch any dripping sauce.

Kids' Favorite Fondue

SERVES 6

• • • • •

Thanks to my dear friend, Marilyn Linton, writer, editor and volunteer extraordinaire, for this oh-so-easy "fondue." Creamy and delicious, it is a great hit with adults as well as kids. Give everyone their own fondue fork and serve with thick slices of French baguette, quartered, celery sticks or slices of green pepper.

• • • • •

Tips

If you're in a hurry, bring the tomatoes to a boil on top of the stove after they have been processed. Then transfer to the slow cooker.

Large cans of tomatoes come in 28 oz (796 mL) and 35 oz (980 mL) sizes. For convenience, I've called for the 28 oz (796 mL) size in my recipes. If you're using the 35 oz (980 mL) size, drain off 1 cup (250 mL) liquid before adding to recipe.

• Works best in a small (maximum 3½ quart) slow cooker
• Fondue forks

1	large can (28 oz/796 mL) tomatoes including juice (see Tips, left)	1
1 tsp	dried oregano leaves	5 mL
1 tsp	salt	5 mL
¼ tsp	freshly ground black pepper	1 mL
3 cups	shredded Cheddar cheese	750 mL
	Sliced baguette	
	Celery sticks	
	Sliced green pepper	

1. In a food processor or blender, process tomatoes with juice until relatively smooth. Transfer to slow cooker stoneware. Add oregano, salt and pepper and cook on **High** for 1 hour, until tomatoes are bubbling hot.

2. Add cheese to slow cooker in handfuls, stirring to combine after each addition. Reduce heat to **Low** and serve, or cover and keep on **Low** until ready to serve. Using fondue forks, dip bread or vegetables into fondue.

Mushroom and Roasted Garlic Crostini page 26 ➤

Classic Swiss Fondue

SERVES 6 TO 8 AS AN APPETIZER

• • • • • •

This is the mother of all fondues — thick and luscious cheese with an intriguing hint of kirsch, an aromatic cherry eau de vie. It's wonderfully welcoming after a day in the cold. If you live in an area that receives lots of snow, think about initiating a tradition of serving fondue on the day of the first snowfall, as some of our friends do.

• • • • • •

Tip

One secret to getting a Swiss fondue to work in a slow cooker is to ensure that the wine is boiling before you add the cheese. Benefits to making a fondue in the slow cooker are that it keeps the mixture at the right temperature and eliminates concern about keeping a flame lit, often a problem with traditional fondue pots.

• Works best in a small (maximum 3½ quart) slow cooker
• Fondue forks

I	clove garlic, split	I
I lb	Swiss Emmenthal cheese, shredded	500 g
2 tbsp	all-purpose flour	25 mL
2 cups	dry white wine	500 mL
¼ cup	kirsch	50 mL
	Freshly grated nutmeg	
	Sliced baguette	

1. Rub slow cooker stoneware with garlic. Cover and turn heat to **High**.

2. On a large plate or platter, combine cheese and flour, using your hands to ensure that flour is distributed as evenly as possible. Set aside.

3. In a saucepan, over medium heat, bring wine to a rapid boil (see Tip, left). Pour into slow cooker stoneware. Add cheese mixture in handfuls, stirring to thoroughly combine after each addition. When all the cheese has been added, cover and cook on **High** for 30 minutes, until cheese is melted and mixture is hot. Add kirsch and stir to combine. Grate fresh nutmeg over mixture and turn heat to **Low**.

4. Break baguette slices into halves or quarters and, using fondue forks, dip into the hot cheese.

◄ Black Bean and Salsa Dip *page 29*

Spinach Soufflé with Horseradish Cream

SERVES 4

• • • • •

This isn't really a soufflé — it's a custard — but its light texture reminds me of those airy delights. This makes a great brunch or light lunch served with a salad of sliced tomatoes.

• • • • •

Tip

I make this in a 7-inch (17.5 cm) square dish. If you vary the dimensions of the dish, the cooking times will also vary. The custard will cook more quickly in a dish with larger dimensions.

• Lightly greased 4-cup (1 L) baking dish

8 oz	fresh spinach leaves or 1 package (10 oz/300 g) spinach, washed, stems removed and coarsely chopped	250 g
1 tbsp	butter	15 mL
1/4 cup	finely chopped onion	50 mL
1	clove garlic, minced	1
1/2 tsp	salt	2 mL
1/4 tsp	black pepper	1 mL
1 tsp	Dijon mustard	5 mL
3/4 cup	half-and-half (10%) cream	175 mL
1/2 cup	shredded mozzarella cheese	125 mL
2	eggs, beaten	2

HORSERADISH CREAM

1/4 cup	whipping (35%) cream	50 mL
2 tbsp	prepared horseradish	10 mL

1. In a large pot of boiling salted water, cook spinach until just wilted. Place in a colander to thoroughly drain, chop coarsely, then transfer to a mixing bowl and set aside.

2. In a skillet, melt butter over medium heat. Add onion and cook, stirring, until softened, about 3 minutes. Add garlic, salt and pepper and cook, stirring, for 1 minute. Add mustard and cream and stir to combine. Add cheese and cook, stirring, until melted.

3. In a bowl, mix together cheese mixture and spinach. Fold eggs into mixture and turn into prepared baking dish. Cover with foil and tie securely with string. Place in slow cooker stoneware and pour in enough boiling water to reach 1 inch (2.5 cm) up the sides of dish. Cover and cook on **High** for $2\frac{1}{2}$ to 3 hours, until set.

4. Horseradish Cream: Whip cream until thick and blend in horseradish. Serve each serving of spinach soufflé with a dollop of horseradish cream.

Cheese Loaves with Mushroom Tomato Sauce

SERVES 6 AS A STARTER OR 4 AS A LIGHT MEAL

• • • • • •

This is a versatile and delicious dish. Serve it as a starter to an elegant meal or as the centerpiece of a light dinner or lunch. If using canned tomatoes, use good-quality Italian tomatoes, such as San Marzano, for the sauce.

• • • • • •

Tip

Many supermarkets stock mini loaf pans among their selection of foil baking pans.

• 2 mini loaf pans (6 by 3 inches/15 by 7.5 cm), lightly greased

CHEESE LOAVES

2 cups	table (18%) cream	500 mL
2	eggs	2
2	egg yolks	2
½ tsp	paprika	2 mL
½ tsp	salt	2 mL
¼ tsp	freshly ground black pepper	1 mL
¾ cup	freshly grated Parmesan cheese	175 mL

MUSHROOM TOMATO SAUCE

2 tbsp	butter	25 mL
8 oz	cremini mushrooms, sliced	250 g
½ tsp	salt	2 mL
¼ tsp	freshly ground black pepper	1 mL
¼ tsp	dried oregano leaves	1 mL
4	green onions, white part only, finely chopped	4
2 cups	tomatoes, peeled and diced or 1 can (28 oz/796 mL) tomatoes, drained and chopped	500 mL

1. **Cheese Loaves:** In a bowl, whisk cream with eggs and egg yolks until well integrated. Whisk in paprika, salt and black pepper. Stir in cheese. Divide mixture equally between prepared pans. Cover with foil and tie with string. Place in slow cooker stoneware and pour in enough boiling water to come 1 inch (2.5 cm) up the sides. Cover and cook on **High** for 3 hours or until a knife inserted in loaf comes out clean.

2. **Mushroom Tomato Sauce:** In a skillet, melt butter over medium heat. Add mushrooms and cook, stirring, until they release their liquid. Add salt, black pepper and oregano and cook, stirring, for 1 minute. Add onions and tomatoes and cook, stirring frequently, until sauce thickens.

3. When ready to serve, remove foil from loaf pans, run a sharp knife around the loaves and invert onto a large platter. Spoon sauce over loaves and serve.

Savory Bread Pudding

SERVES ABOUT 6

• • • • •

What could be more inviting than this mouth-watering combination of tomatoes, cheese and milk with hints of mustard and onion? It makes a delicious supper or brunch dish, served with a simple green salad. As a bonus, it's a great way to use up day-old bread.

• • • • •

Tip

Tea towels prevent accumulated moisture from dripping on the bread by absorbing whatever is generated during cooking.

• Lightly greased slow cooker stoneware

I tbsp	vegetable oil	15 mL
I	onion, halved and thinly sliced on the vertical	I
4	cloves garlic, thinly sliced	4
2 tsp	dried Italian seasoning	10 mL
I tsp	salt	5 mL
½ tsp	cracked black peppercorns	2 mL
I	can (28 oz/796 mL) tomatoes, including juice, coarsely chopped	I
4	eggs, beaten	4
I tbsp	Dijon mustard	15 mL
2 cups	evaporated milk	500 mL
8 cups	cubed (½-inch/I cm) country-style bread (about half a large Calabrese loaf)	2 L
2 cups	shredded Fontina cheese	500 mL

1. In a skillet, heat oil over medium heat. Add onion and cook, stirring, until softened, about 3 minutes. Add garlic, dried Italian seasoning, salt and peppercorns and cook, stirring, for 1 minute. Add tomatoes with juice and bring to a boil. Remove from heat and set aside.

2. In a bowl, combine eggs and mustard. Beat to blend. Add evaporated milk and beat well. Set aside.

3. In prepared stoneware, spoon one-third of tomato mixture. Spread half the bread evenly over top and sprinkle bread evenly with half the cheese. Repeat, finishing with final third of tomato mixture. Pour milk mixture evenly over the top.

4. Place two clean tea towels, each folded in half (so you will have four layers), over top of stoneware, to absorb the moisture (see Tip, left). Cover and cook on **Low** for 6 hours or **High** for 3 hours, until pudding is set and edges are browning.

Soups

Vegetable Stock

**MAKES ABOUT
8 CUPS (2 L)**

• • • • •

This recipe produces a mildly flavored stock that will not overpower the taste of most vegetable recipes. If you prefer a stronger-tasting stock, after straining off the liquid, transfer to a stockpot and simmer, uncovered, for 30 minutes until it is reduced by about one-third or use Roasted or Enhanced Vegetable Stock (see Variations, right).

• • • • •

Tip

There are few firm rules about what vegetables to include in stock. Making stock is a good way to use up the parts of vegetables that are usually discarded, such as the green part of scallions or leeks, which can be substituted for onions, or mushroom stems, which add depth and flavor. However, the vegetables must be in good condition. Do not use any that have passed their peak. Moreover, vegetables from the cruciferous family, which includes broccoli, cabbage and turnip, should not be used as their pungency will overpower the other ingredients.

8 cups	water	2 L
4	stalks celery, coarsely chopped	4
4	carrots, scrubbed and coarsely chopped	4
2	onions, coarsely chopped	2
2	cloves garlic	2
4	sprigs parsley	4
2	bay leaves	2
½ tsp	salt	2 mL
8	black peppercorns	8

1. In slow cooker stoneware, combine water, celery, carrots, onions, garlic, parsley, bay leaves, salt and peppercorns. Cover and cook on **Low** for 8 hours or on **High** for 4 hours. Strain and discard solids. Cover and refrigerate for up to 5 days or freeze in an airtight container.

Variations

Roasted Vegetable Stock

Preheat oven to 425°F (220°C). In a bowl, toss celery, carrots, onions and garlic in 1 tbsp (15 mL) olive oil. Spread on a baking sheet and roast, turning 3 or 4 times, for 20 minutes, until nicely browned. Transfer to slow cooker stoneware, add remaining ingredients and proceed with recipe.

Enhanced Vegetable Stock

To enhance 8 cups (2 L) prepared or basic vegetable stock, combine in a large saucepan over medium heat with 2 carrots, peeled and coarsely chopped, 1 tbsp (15 mL) tomato paste, 1 tsp (5 mL) celery seed, 1 tsp (5 mL) cracked black peppercorns, ½ tsp (2 mL) dried thyme leaves, 4 parsley sprigs, 1 bay leaf and 1 cup (250 mL) white wine. Bring to a boil. Reduce heat to low and simmer, covered, for 30 minutes, then strain and discard solids.

French Onion Soup

SERVES 6

On a chilly day, there's nothing more appetizing than a bowl of steaming hot onion soup, bubbling away under a blanket of browned cheese. Normally, caramelizing the onions for this masterpiece is a laborious process that can easily involve an hour of almost constant stirring. Fortunately, your slow cooker can now do most of this tiresome work for you.

Tip

Since it's important that the stock for this soup be very flavorful, I recommend using Enhanced Vegetable Stock. The results are more than worth the added effort. This is one of the best onion soups ever!

- 6 ovenproof soup bowls
- Preheated broiler

3 lbs	sliced onions (about 6 medium onions)	1.5 kg
2 tbsp	melted butter	25 mL
1 tbsp	granulated sugar	15 mL
1 tsp	salt	5 mL
1 tsp	cracked black peppercorns	5 mL
8 cups	Enhanced Vegetable Stock (see recipe, page 38)	2 L
2 tbsp	brandy or cognac (optional)	25 mL
12	slices baguette, about ½ inch (1 cm) thick	12
2 cups	shredded Swiss or Gruyère cheese	500 mL

1. In slow cooker stoneware, combine onions and butter. Stir to coat onions thoroughly. Cover and cook on **High** for 1 hour, until onions are softened.

2. Add sugar, salt and peppercorns and stir well. Place two clean tea towels, each folded in half (so you will have four layers), over top of stoneware, to absorb the moisture. Cover and cook on **High** for 4 hours, stirring two or three times to ensure that onions are browning evenly, replacing towels each time.

3. Add vegetable stock and brandy, if using. Remove towels, cover and cook on **High** for 2 hours.

4. Preheat broiler. Ladle soup into ovenproof bowls. Place 2 slices baguette in each bowl. Sprinkle liberally with cheese and broil for 2 to 3 minutes, until top is bubbling and brown. Serve immediately.

Pumpkin Soup with Lime

SERVES 6 TO 8

· · · · ·

This soup, which is delicious hot or cold, has its origins in both French provincial and Latin American cuisine. It's breathtakingly easy and makes an elegant start to any meal. If pumpkin is unavailable, substitute any orange-fleshed squash, such as acorn or butternut.

· · · · ·

Tips

If using pumpkin seeds, panfry in a dry, hot skillet until they are lightly browned and puffed. When purchasing pumpkin seeds, taste first, as they tend to go rancid quickly. Store in the freezer until ready for use.

If substituting squash for pumpkin, try the frozen diced version for convenience.

· · · · ·

Make ahead

This soup can be assembled the night before it is cooked. Complete Step 1. The next morning continue cooking as directed.

6 cups	peeled pumpkin, cut into 2-inch (5 cm) cubes	1.5 L
3	leeks, white part only, cleaned and coarsely chopped (see Tip, page 41)	3
4 cups	vegetable stock	1 L
1 tsp	salt	5 mL
1/4 tsp	freshly ground black pepper	1 mL
	Zest and juice of 1 lime	
Pinch	cayenne pepper	Pinch
1 cup	whipping (35%) cream	250 mL
6 to 8	cherry tomatoes, halved	6 to 8
1/4 cup	toasted pumpkin seeds (optional) (see Tips, left)	50 mL
	Finely chopped chives or cilantro	

1. In slow cooker stoneware, combine pumpkin, leeks, stock, salt and black pepper.

2. Cover and cook on **Low** for 8 to 10 hours or on **High** for 4 to 6 hours, until pumpkin is tender. Strain vegetables, reserving stock. In a blender or food processor, purée vegetables with 1 cup (250 mL) reserved stock until smooth. Or, using a hand-held blender, purée the soup in stoneware.

3. If serving hot, return soup to slow cooker, add remaining stock, lime zest and juice, cayenne and cream and cook on **High** for 20 minutes. If serving cold, combine ingredients in a large bowl and chill thoroughly.

4. When ready to serve, ladle soup into individual bowls and garnish with cherry tomatoes, pumpkin seeds, if using, and chives or cilantro.

Creamy Leek Soup with Stilton

SERVES 6 TO 8

• • • • •

This English version of a classic French leek and potato soup is a quintessential winter dish.

• • • • •

Tips

To clean leeks: Fill sink full of lukewarm water. Split leeks in half lengthwise and submerge in water, swishing them around to remove all traces of dirt. Transfer to a colander and rinse under cold water.

If you're in a hurry, you can soften the leeks and onion in a skillet over medium heat. Melt the butter and cook, stirring until softened, about 4 minutes. Stir in garlic, salt and pepper. Transfer to slow cooker and continue as directed.

• • • • •

Make ahead

To serve hot, complete Step 1 and refrigerate overnight. The next morning continue with the recipe.

To serve cold as Vichyssoise: Cook soup overnight in slow cooker. Purée in morning and chill until ready to serve. Continue as directed.

2 tbsp	melted butter	15 mL
6 cups	leeks, white part with about 2 inches (5 cm) green, about 5 medium leeks cleaned and coarsely chopped	1.5 L
1 cup	chopped onion	250 mL
2 tbsp	finely chopped garlic	25 mL
1 tsp	salt	5 mL
1/4 tsp	freshly ground black pepper	1 mL
3 cups	potatoes, peeled and cut into 1/2-inch (1 cm) cubes	750 mL
6 cups	vegetable stock	1.5 L
1 cup	whipping (35%) cream	250 mL
8 oz	Stilton cheese	250 g

1. In slow cooker stoneware, combine leeks, onion, garlic, salt, pepper and melted butter. Stir to coat vegetables thoroughly. Cover and cook on **High** for 30 minutes to 1 hour, until vegetables are softened. Add potatoes and vegetable stock.

2. Cover and cook on **Low** for 8 to 10 hours or on **High** for 4 to 6 hours, until vegetables are tender.

3. In a blender or food processor, purée soup in batches. Or, using a hand-held blender, purée the soup in stoneware. Ladle into bowls. Drizzle with whipping cream and top each serving with about 2 heaping tbsp (25 mL) Stilton. Serve immediately.

Variations

Vichyssoise
Omit stilton. Reduce the quantity of leeks to 3 cups (750 mL) and increase the quantity of potatoes to 5 cups (1.25 L). After the soup is puréed, transfer to a large bowl and chill thoroughly. Before serving, stir in cream. Spoon into individual soup bowls and garnish with finely chopped chives.

Watercress Vichyssoise
Add one bunch watercress to mixture when puréeing. Serve soup garnished with chopped watercress.

Cranberry Borscht

SERVES 6 TO 8

• • • • •

Served cold in chilled bowls, this fresh, fruity soup is one of my favorite preludes to an outdoor dinner on a warm night. My friend, Margret Hovanec, calls this a summer borscht, made without meat from garden-fresh beets, and I thank her for the idea of enhancing the stock with beet leaves. Many years ago, I learned about adding cranberries to borscht from a recipe created by New York restaurateur George Lang. Their fruity tang provides just enough tartness to round out the soup. This soup is also good served hot.

• • • • •

Make ahead

This dish can be assembled the night before it is cooked but without adding the cranberries, sugar, orange juice and zest and beet leaves. Complete Step 1 and cover and refrigerate overnight. The next day, continue cooking as directed in Step 2. Or the soup can be cooked overnight in the slow cooker, finished the next morning and chilled during the day.

6	medium beets, peeled and cut into ½-inch (1 cm) cubes	6
	Leaves from the beets, washed, coarsely chopped and set aside in refrigerator	
4	cloves garlic, chopped	4
5 cups	Enhanced Vegetable Stock (see recipe, page 38)	1.25 L
1 tsp	salt	5 mL
½ tsp	freshly ground black pepper	2 mL
1 cup	cranberries	250 mL
2 tbsp	granulated sugar	25 mL
	Zest and juice of 1 orange	
	Sour cream (optional)	
	Chopped dill (optional)	

1. In slow cooker stoneware, combine beets, garlic, stock, water, salt and pepper.

2. Cover and cook on **Low** for 8 to 10 hours or on **High** for 4 to 5 hours, until vegetables are tender. Add cranberries, sugar, orange zest and juice and beet leaves. Cover and cook on **High** for 30 minutes or until cranberries are popping from their skins.

3. In a blender or food processor, purée soup in batches. Or, using a hand-held blender, purée the soup in stoneware. If serving cold, transfer to a large bowl and chill thoroughly, preferably overnight.

4. When ready to serve, spoon into individual bowls, top with sour cream and garnish with dill, if using.

Sophisticated Mushroom Barley Soup

SERVES 6 TO 8

• • • • •

Dried wild mushrooms give this soup a rich flavor and sophisticated flair. At the same time, it's hearty enough to make an ideal pick-me-up after a busy day. Spiff it up by adding ½ cup (125 mL) sherry or Madeira just before serving.

• • • • •

Tip

For a more flavorful soup, use Roasted or Enhanced Vegetable Stock (see recipes, page 38) in this recipe.

• • • • •

Make ahead

This dish can be assembled the night before it is cooked. Follow preparation directions in Steps 1 and 2 and refrigerate overnight. The next day, continue cooking as directed in Step 3.

I cup	boiling water	250 mL
I	package (½ oz/14 g) dried wild mushrooms, such as porcini	I
2 tbsp	vegetable oil or butter, divided	25 mL
3	onions, finely chopped	3
6	cloves garlic, minced	6
I tsp	salt	5 mL
I tsp	cracked black peppercorns	5 mL
I ½ lbs	button mushrooms, sliced	750 g
⅔ cup	pearl barley	150 mL
7 cups	vegetable stock (see Tip, left)	1.75 L
I	bay leaf	I
¼ cup	soy sauce	50 mL
	Finely chopped green onions or parsley (optional)	

1. In a heatproof bowl, combine boiling water and dried mushrooms. Let stand for 30 minutes, then strain through a fine sieve, reserving liquid. Chop mushrooms finely and set aside.

2. In a skillet, over medium heat, heat 1 tbsp (15 mL) vegetable oil. Add onions and cook, stirring, for 3 minutes, until softened. Add garlic, salt and peppercorns and cook for 1 minute. Transfer mixture to slow cooker stoneware. In same pan, heat remaining oil and cook button mushrooms over medium-high heat just until they begin to lose their liquid. Add dried mushrooms, toss to combine and cook for 1 minute. Transfer mixture to slow cooker stoneware. Add barley, reserved mushroom soaking liquid, stock, bay leaf and soy sauce.

3. Cover and cook on **Low** for 6 to 8 hours or on **High** for 3 to 4 hours. Discard bay leaf. Ladle into individual bowls and garnish with chopped green onions or parsley, if using.

Sumptuous Celery Soup

SERVES 6 TO 8

Celeriac, or celery root, is actually a type of celery, with crispy white flesh that is slightly peppery. Since it will keep for a week or longer in the refrigerator, it makes an excellent winter vegetable. This simple cream soup has a sweet, yet piquant flavor, which responds to the addition of dill. Serve it as a starter to an elegant dinner or as a weekday meal with crusty bread and salad.

Tip

Since celery root oxidizes quickly on contact with air, be sure to use as soon as it is shredded, or toss with 1 tbsp (15 mL) lemon juice to prevent discoloration.

Make ahead

This soup can be assembled the night before it is cooked, but without adding the cream, nutmeg and dill. Follow preparation directions in Step 1 and refrigerate overnight. The next day, continue cooking as directed in Step 2.

1 tbsp	butter	15 mL
1	medium onion, chopped	1
1	clove garlic, minced	1
1/2 tsp	salt	2 mL
1/4 tsp	freshly ground black pepper	1 mL
1	large celery root, peeled and shredded (see Tip, left)	1
1	large potato, peeled and cut into 1/2-inch (1 cm) cubes	1
4 cups	vegetable stock	1 L
1 cup	whipping (35%) cream	250 mL
Pinch	ground nutmeg	Pinch
1/4 cup	chopped fresh dill	50 mL

1. In a skillet, melt butter over medium heat. Add onion and cook, stirring, for 3 minutes, until softened. Add garlic, salt and pepper and cook for 1 minute. Add celery root and potato, stirring to combine. Pour stock over mixture.

2. Transfer to slow cooker stoneware. Cover and cook on **Low** for 8 to 10 hours or on **High** for 4 to 5 hours, until vegetables are tender.

3. Using a slotted spoon, transfer solids plus 1 cup (250 mL) liquid to a blender or food processor and process until smooth. Or, using a hand-held blender, purée the soup in stoneware. Return to slow cooker, add cream and nutmeg. Cover and cook on **High** for 15 minutes. Ladle soup into bowls and garnish with dill.

Southwestern Corn and Roasted Red Pepper Soup

SERVES 6

• • • • •

Although the roots of this soup lie deep in the heart of Tex-Mex cuisine, it is elegant enough for even the most gracious occasion. Serve it as a starter or as a deliciously different meal-in-a-bowl. Hot sourdough bread makes a perfect accompaniment.

• • • • •

Tips

Dried New Mexico chilies are available in most supermarkets. Their smoky flavor adds a nice note to this soup, but you can omit them and add a smoky hot pepper sauce, such as one made with chipotle peppers, to taste, after the soup is cooked.

Use bottled roasted red peppers for convenience.

• • • • •

Make ahead

This dish can be assembled the night before it is cooked but without adding the roasted pepper and whipping cream. Complete Steps 1 and 2 and refrigerate. The next day, continue with Step 3.

1	dried New Mexico chili (optional) (see Tips, right)	1
1 cup	boiling water	250 mL
1	large onion, diced	1
6	cloves garlic, minced	6
1 tbsp	cumin seeds (see Tips, page 50)	15 mL
1 tbsp	chopped rosemary, dried or fresh	15 mL
6 cups	vegetable stock	1.5 L
1	bay leaf	1
1 tsp	salt	5 mL
½ tsp	freshly ground black pepper	2 mL
4 cups	corn kernels	1 L
2	roasted red bell peppers, cut into ½-inch (1 cm) cubes (see Tips, page 29)	2
2 cups	whipping (35%) cream	500 mL
	Finely chopped parsley or cilantro	

1. In a heatproof bowl, soak chili pepper in boiling water for 30 minutes. Drain.

2. In a blender or food processor, purée chili, onion, garlic, cumin seeds and rosemary with ½ cup (125 mL) stock. Add to slow cooker stoneware along with remaining stock, bay leaf, salt, black pepper and corn.

3. Cover and cook on **Low** for 6 to 8 hours or on **High** for 3 to 4 hours.

4. Add roasted pepper and whipping cream. Cover and cook on **High** for 15 to 20 minutes, until heated through. Discard bay leaf. Spoon into individual bowls and garnish with parsley or cilantro.

Caribbean Pepper Pot Soup

SERVES 6

• • • • •

This delicious vegetable soup is a meal in itself and it's so good, you'll want seconds. I particularly like the way the sweetness of the brown sugar and the coconut milk combines with the heat of the chili.

• • • • •

Tips

Although any chili pepper will provide heat, only Scotch bonnet peppers, available in West Indian markets, truly capture the flavor of the Caribbean. Short, squat and slightly wrinkled and ranging in color from yellow to red to green, Scotch bonnets have a unique smoky flavor. Be particularly cautious when handling them, as they are reputedly the world's hottest pepper. A Habanero pepper will produce a similar result.

For convenience, use frozen, chopped butternut squash.

An easy way to coarsely chop tomatoes while in the can is to use a table knife. Hold the knife vertically in the can and move from side to side, breaking up the tomatoes.

1 tbsp	vegetable oil	15 mL
2	onions, finely chopped	2
4	stalks celery, peeled and thinly sliced	4
4	cloves garlic, minced	4
1 tbsp	minced gingerroot	15 mL
2 tbsp	chili powder	25 mL
1 tsp	whole coriander seeds, crushed (see Tips, right)	5 mL
1 tsp	salt	5 mL
1 tsp	cracked black peppercorns	5 mL
1 tbsp	packed brown sugar	15 mL
4 cups	acorn or butternut squash, peeled and cut into ½-inch (1 cm) cubes, or 4 cups (1 L) carrots, peeled and thinly sliced	1 L
1	can (14 to 19 oz/398 to 540 mL) kidney beans, rinsed and drained, or 2 cups (500 mL) dried kidney beans, cooked and drained	1
1	can (28 oz/796 mL) tomatoes, including juice, chopped (see Tips, left)	1
4 cups	vegetable stock	1 L
1	green bell pepper, diced	1
½ to 1	chili pepper, preferably Scotch bonnet, finely chopped (see Tips, left)	½ to 1
1	can (14 oz/398 mL) coconut milk	1
	Finely chopped parsley or cilantro (optional)	

1. In a large skillet, heat oil over medium heat. Add onions and celery and cook, stirring, until softened, about 5 minutes. Add garlic, gingerroot, chili powder, coriander seeds, salt and peppercorns and cook, stirring, for 1 minute. Add sugar and stir to combine. Add squash or carrots, kidney beans, tomatoes with juice and stock.

I like to use crushed whole coriander seeds in this recipe, as they release their flavor slowly as the soup cooks. I do this in a mortar, but you could also use a spice grinder. Failing that, use ½ tsp (2 mL) ground coriander.

• • • • •

Make ahead

This soup can be assembled in advance of serving, but without adding the chili pepper and coconut milk. Complete Step 1 and refrigerate overnight. The next day, continue cooking as directed in Step 2.

2. Transfer to slow cooker stoneware. Cover and cook on **Low** for 8 to 10 hours or on **High** for 4 to 5 hours, until vegetables are tender.

3. Add green pepper, chili pepper and coconut milk. Cover and cook on **High** for another 15 to 20 minutes, until heated through. Garnish with parsley or cilantro, if using.

Mulligatawny Soup

SERVES 8

• • • • •

Mulligatawny, which means "pepper water" in Tamil, is an Anglo-Indian soup, imported to England by seafaring merchants. It is usually made with chicken, but a vegetarian version was documented by the great English cook Eliza Acton in her book *Modern Cookery*, published in 1845. Using potatoes rather than rice is a departure from the norm as is the option of adding cauliflower. This is a hearty and tasty soup that is suitable for many occasions, either as a first course or the focal point of a light meal.

• • • • •

Make ahead

This soup can be partially prepared the night before it is cooked. Complete Step 1. Cover and refrigerate mixture overnight. The next morning, continue cooking as directed in Step 2.

1 tbsp	vegetable oil	15 mL
2	onions, finely chopped	2
2	carrots, peeled and thinly sliced	2
4	stalks celery, peeled and thinly sliced	4
4	cloves garlic, minced	4
1 tbsp	curry powder	15 mL
1 tsp	cumin seeds	5 mL
1 tsp	salt	5 mL
½ tsp	cracked black peppercorns	2 mL
2	medium potatoes, peeled and diced	2
5 cups	vegetable stock	1.25 L
1 cup	whipping (35%) cream or plain yogurt	250 mL
2 cups	cauliflower florets, thawed if frozen (optional)	500 mL
	Finely chopped cilantro or parsley	

1. In a skillet, heat oil over medium heat. Add onions, carrots and celery and cook, stirring, for 7 minutes, until softened. Add garlic, curry powder, cumin seeds, salt and peppercorns and cook, stirring, for 1 minute. Add potatoes and stock and bring to a boil. Transfer to slow cooker stoneware.

2. Cover and cook on **Low** for 8 to 10 hours or on **High** for 4 to 5 hours, until vegetables are tender. In a blender or food processor, purée soup in batches and return to slow cooker stoneware. Or, using a hand-held blender, purée the soup in stoneware. Stir in cream and cauliflower, if using. Cover and cook on **High** for 30 minutes, until cauliflower is tender.

3. When ready to serve, ladle into bowls and garnish with cilantro or parsley.

South American Black Bean Soup

SERVES 4 TO 6 AS A MAIN COURSE OR 6 TO 8 AS A STARTER

• • • • •

This mouth-watering combination of black beans, lime juice and cilantro with just a hint of hot pepper is one of my favorite one-dish meals. To jack up the heat, add the jalapeño. The flavor of this soup actually improves if it is allowed to sit overnight and then reheated.

• • • • •

Tips

If you prefer a spicier version of this dish, garnish with extra fiery salsa.

For a more flavorful result, use Roasted or Enhanced Vegetable Stock (see recipes, page 38).

• • • • •

Make ahead

This dish can be assembled the night before it is cooked but without adding the lime juice and garnishes. Complete Step 1. Cover and refrigerate overnight. The next day, continue cooking as directed in Step 2.

1 tbsp	vegetable oil	15 mL
2	onions, finely chopped	2
2	stalks celery, peeled and finely chopped	2
2	carrots, peeled and finely chopped	2
2	cloves garlic, minced	2
1	finely chopped jalapeño pepper (optional)	1
1 tsp	dried thyme leaves	5 mL
2 tbsp	cumin seeds	25 mL
1 tbsp	dried oregano leaves	15 mL
1 tsp	salt	5 mL
1 tsp	cracked black peppercorns	5 mL
1/4 tsp	cayenne pepper	1 mL
2 tbsp	tomato paste	25 mL
6 cups	vegetable stock	1.5 L
2	cans black beans, rinsed and drained (each 14 to 19 oz/398 to 540 mL), or 2 cups (500 mL) dried black beans, cooked and drained	2
1/3 cup	freshly squeezed lime juice	75 mL
	Finely chopped cilantro	
	Sour cream (optional)	
	Salsa (optional)	

1. In a skillet, heat oil over medium heat. Add onions, celery and carrots and cook, stirring, until vegetables are softened, about 5 minutes. Add garlic, jalapeño, if using, thyme, cumin seeds, oregano, salt, peppercorns and cayenne and cook, stirring, for 1 minute. Add tomato paste and stir to combine. Transfer contents of pan to slow cooker stoneware. Add vegetable stock and beans and stir to combine.

2. Cover and cook on **Low** for 8 to 10 hours or on **High** for 4 to 6 hours.

3. Before serving, stir in lime juice. In blender or food processor, purée soup in batches. Spoon into individual soup bowls and garnish with cilantro and/or sour cream and salsa, if using.

Red Lentil and Carrot Soup with Coconut

SERVES 8 TO 10 AS A STARTER OR 4 TO 6 AS A MAIN COURSE

good

I love the combination of flavors in this unusual soup. The red lentils partially dissolve while cooking, creating a creamy texture and the coconut milk creates an intriguing, almost nutty note. Serve as a starter or add an Indian bread and salad for a delicious light meal.

Tips

If you don't have fresh chili peppers, stir in your favorite hot pepper sauce, to taste, just before serving.

For an enhanced cumin flavor, toast the cumin seeds and coarsely crush (see page 124) before using in this recipe.

Make ahead

This soup can be partially prepared the night before it is cooked. Complete Steps 1 and 2. Cover and refrigerate overnight. The next day, continue cooking as directed in Step 3.

2 cups	red lentils	500 mL
1 tbsp	vegetable oil	15 mL
2	onions, finely chopped	2
2	large carrots, peeled, cut in half lengthwise and thinly sliced	2
4	cloves garlic, minced	4
2 tsp	turmeric	10 mL
2 tsp	cumin seeds (see Tips, left)	10 mL
1 tsp	salt	5 mL
1/2 tsp	cracked black peppercorns	2 mL
1	can (28 oz/796 mL) tomatoes, including juice	1
6 cups	vegetable stock	1.5 L
1	can (14 oz/398 mL) coconut milk	1
1 tbsp	freshly squeezed lemon juice	15 mL
1	long red chili pepper or 2 Thai chilies, finely chopped (see Tips, left)	1
	Thin slices lemon (optional)	
	Finely chopped cilantro (optional)	

No chilies for Shane

1. In a colander, rinse lentils thoroughly under cold running water. Set aside.

2. In a skillet, heat oil over medium heat. Add onions and carrots and cook, stirring, until softened, about 5 minutes. Add garlic, turmeric, cumin seeds, salt and peppercorns and cook, stirring, for 1 minute. Add tomatoes with juice and bring to a boil, breaking up with the back of a spoon. Stir in reserved lentils and stock.

3. Transfer mixture to slow cooker stoneware. Cover and cook on **Low** for 8 to 10 hours or on **High** for 4 to 5 hours, until carrots are tender and mixture is bubbling. Stir in coconut milk, lemon juice and chili pepper and cook on **High** for 20 to 30 minutes, until heated through.

4. When ready to serve, ladle into bowls and top with lemon slices and cilantro, if using.

Mediterranean Lentil Soup with Spinach

SERVES 6 TO 8

• • • • •

This delicious soup, delicately flavored with lemon and cumin, reminds me of hot, languid days under the Mediterranean sun. Serve it as a starter or add a green salad and warm country-style bread for a refreshing and nutritious light meal.

• • • • •

Tip

For an enhanced cumin flavor, toast the cumin seeds and coarsely crush (see page 124) before using in this recipe.

• • • • •

Make ahead

This soup can be partially prepared the night before it is cooked, but without adding the spinach and lemon juice. Complete Steps 1 and 2. Cover and refrigerate overnight. The next day, continue cooking as directed in Step 3.

1 cup	green or brown lentils	250 mL
1 tbsp	vegetable oil	15 mL
2	onions, chopped	2
2	stalks celery, peeled and chopped	2
2	large carrots, peeled and chopped	2
1	clove garlic, minced	1
1 tsp	cumin seeds (see Tip, left)	5 mL
1 tsp	grated lemon zest	5 mL
1	potato, peeled and grated	1
6 cups	vegetable stock	1.5 L
8 oz	fresh spinach leaves, washed and coarsely chopped or 1 package (10 oz/300 g) frozen spinach, thawed	250 g
2 tbsp	freshly squeezed lemon juice	25 mL

1. In a colander, rinse lentils thoroughly under cold running water. Set aside.

2. In a skillet, heat oil over medium heat. Add onions, celery and carrots and cook, stirring, until vegetables are softened, about 5 minutes. Add garlic, cumin seeds and lemon zest and cook, stirring for 1 minute. Transfer mixture to slow cooker stoneware. Add reserved lentils, potato and stock.

2. Cover and cook on **Low** for 8 to 10 hours or on **High** for 4 to 6 hours, until vegetables are tender. Add spinach and lemon juice. Cover and cook on **High** for 20 minutes, until spinach is cooked and mixture is hot and bubbling.

Ribollita

SERVES 6 AS A MAIN COURSE OR 8 AS A STARTER

• • • • •

Originally intended as a method for using up leftover minestrone — hence the name ribollita, which means "twice cooked" — this hearty Italian soup has acquired an illustrious reputation of its own. The distinguishing ingredient is country-style bread, which is added to the soup and cooked in the stock. Drizzled with olive oil, this makes a satisfying light meal or tasty starter to an Italian-themed dinner.

• • • • •

Tips

Although I prefer the bit of heat that the chili pepper adds, the soup will be flavorful without it.

If you are not a vegan and have the leftover "boot" of a piece of Parmesan cheese (the tough outer rind), add it to the soup along with the stock for enhanced flavor.

1	can (14 to 19 oz/398 to 540 mL) white kidney beans, drained and rinsed, or 1 cup (250 mL) dried white kidney beans, cooked and drained (see Basic Beans, page 100)	1
5 cups	vegetable stock, divided	1.25 L
1 tbsp	vegetable oil	15 mL
2	onions, finely chopped	2
2	carrots, peeled and diced	2
2	stalks celery, peeled and diced	2
4	cloves garlic, minced	4
1 tbsp	grated lemon zest	15 mL
1 tsp	finely chopped fresh rosemary leaves or dried rosemary leaves, crumbled	5 mL
1 tsp	salt	5 mL
½ tsp	cracked black peppercorns	2 mL
2	potatoes, peeled and grated	2
1	bunch Swiss chard, stems and veins removed and coarsely chopped	1
¼ cup	finely chopped parsley	50 mL
1	long red chili pepper, minced (optional)	1
3	thick slices day-old country-style bread	3
	Extra virgin olive oil	
	Freshly grated Parmesan cheese (optional)	

1. In a food processor, combine beans with 1 cup (250 mL) stock and purée until smooth. Set aside.

2. In a skillet, heat oil over medium heat. Add onions, carrots and celery and cook, stirring, for 7 minutes, until softened. Add garlic, lemon zest, rosemary, salt and peppercorns and cook, stirring, for 1 minute. Add bean mixture and bring to a boil. Stir in potatoes and remaining stock.

Traditionally, ribollita is reheated in the oven. Ladle the soup into ovenproof bowls, drizzle with olive oil and sprinkle with Parmesan, if using. Bake in a preheated oven (350°F/180°C) for 30 minutes, until the top is lightly browned.

• • • • •

Make ahead

Complete Steps 1 and 2 and refrigerate mixture overnight. The next day continue cooking as directed. Or cook the soup overnight or the day before you intend to serve it. Refrigerate until you are ready to serve, then reheat in the oven (see Tip, above).

3. Transfer mixture to slow cooker stoneware. Cover and cook on **Low** for 8 to 10 hours or on **High** for 4 to 5 hours. Stir in Swiss chard, parsley, chili pepper, if using, and bread. Cover and cook on **High** for 30 minutes, until chard is cooked.

4. When ready to serve, ladle into bowls, breaking bread into pieces. Drizzle with extra virgin olive oil and sprinkle with Parmesan, if using.

Santa Fe Sweet Potato Soup

SERVES 6 TO 8

• • • • •

Here's a flavorful, rib-sticking soup with lots of pizzazz and universal appeal. The enticing, slightly smoky flavor of the New Mexico chilies permeates the stock, and the lime, roasted red pepper and cilantro finish provides a nice balance to the sweet potatoes. If you are a heat seeker, add the jalapeño pepper.

• • • • •

Tip

For convenience, use bottled roasted red peppers in this recipe.

• • • • •

Make ahead

This soup can be assembled the night before it is cooked. Follow preparation directions in Steps 1 and 2. Cover and refrigerate overnight. The next day, continue cooking as directed in Steps 3 and 4.

2	dried New Mexico chili peppers	2
2 cups	boiling water	500 mL
1 tbsp	vegetable oil	15 mL
2	onions, finely chopped	2
4	cloves garlic, minced	4
1 tsp	salt	5 mL
1 tsp	dried oregano leaves	5 mL
4 cups	peeled, cubed sweet potatoes, about ½ inch (1 cm)	1 L
6 cups	vegetable stock	1.5 L
2 cups	corn kernels, thawed if frozen	500 mL
1	finely chopped jalapeño pepper (optional)	1
1 tsp	grated lime zest	5 mL
2 tbsp	freshly squeezed lime juice	25 mL
2	roasted red peppers, cut into thin strips (see Tips, page 29)	2
	Finely chopped cilantro	

1. In a heatproof bowl, soak chilies in boiling water for 30 minutes. Drain, discarding soaking liquid and stems. Pat dry, chop finely and set aside.

2. In a skillet, heat oil over medium heat. Add onions and cook, stirring, for 3 minutes, until softened. Add garlic, salt, oregano and reserved chilies and cook, stirring, for 1 minute. Transfer mixture to slow cooker stoneware. Add sweet potatoes and stock and stir to combine.

3. Cover and cook on **Low** for 8 to 10 hours or on **High** for 4 to 6 hours, until sweet potatoes are tender. Strain vegetables, reserving stock. In a blender or food processor, purée vegetables with 1 cup (250 mL) reserved stock until smooth. Return mixture, along with reserved stock, to slow cooker stoneware. Or, using a hand-held blender, purée the soup in stoneware. Add corn, jalapeño pepper, if using, lime zest and juice. Cover and cook on **High** for 20 minutes, until corn is tender.

4. When ready to serve, ladle soup into individual bowls and garnish with red pepper strips and cilantro.

Creamy Corn Chowder

SERVES 6

• • • • •

Here's a comfort food classic that never goes out of style. If you like a bit of spice, add the jalapeño pepper.

• • • • •

Tip

For added flavor, use Roasted Vegetable Stock in this recipe (see recipe, page 38).

• • • • •

Make ahead

This soup can be partially prepared the night before it is cooked. Complete Step 1. Cover and refrigerate overnight. The next morning continue cooking as directed in Step 2.

1 tbsp	vegetable oil	15 mL
2	onions, finely chopped	2
2	stalks celery, peeled and thinly sliced	2
2	carrots, peeled and diced	2
½ tsp	poultry seasoning or dried thyme leaves	2 mL
1 tsp	salt	5 mL
½ tsp	cracked black peppercorns	2 mL
1	bay leaf	1
3½ cups	vegetable stock	875 mL
2	large potatoes, peeled and grated	2
2	cans cream-style corn (each 14 to 19 oz/398 to 540 mL)	2
1	green bell pepper, seeded and finely chopped	1
1	jalapeño pepper, finely chopped (optional)	1
½ tsp	ground cumin	2 mL

1. In a skillet, heat oil over medium heat. Add onions, celery and carrots to pan and cook, stirring, for 7 minutes, until softened. Add poultry seasoning, salt, peppercorns and bay leaf and cook, stirring, for 1 minute. Add stock and bring to a boil. Transfer mixture to slow cooker stoneware. Stir in potatoes.

2. Cover and cook on **Low** for 8 hours or on **High** for 4 hours, until vegetables are tender. Add corn, green pepper, jalapeño, if using, and cumin. Stir well. Cover and cook on **High** for 30 minutes, until soup is hot.

Variation

Creamy Corn Chowder with Cumin Crema

Dress this soup up with a Cumin Crema topping. To make, toast 2 tsp (10 mL) cumin seeds in a dry skillet until they release their aroma. Remove from heat immediately and grind seeds in a spice grinder or in a mortar with a pestle. Whip ½ cup (125 mL) whipping (35%) cream. Fold ground cumin into the whipped cream and top each serving of soup with a dollop of the crema.

Tortilla Soup with Corn and Chilies

SERVES 6

• • • • •

This is my husband's favorite soup. He can't get enough of the smoky broth and the creamy avocados, which make an irresistible combination.

• • • • •

Tips

For maximum flavor, use Enhanced Vegetable Stock (see recipe, page 38) in this soup.

Pinto beans are a medium-size, pinky-beige bean often used in Southwestern and Tex-Mex cooking. They have a unique, smoky flavor that marries well with many chilies. Although they lack the pinto bean's earthiness, red kidney or dried Romano beans may be substituted.

Canned beans are a quick and easy substitute for cooked dried beans. For 2 cups (500 mL) cooked beans, use a standard 19-oz (540 mL) can. Drain and rinse well under cold running water before adding to the recipe.

I	dried New Mexico chili pepper	I
2 cups	boiling water	500 mL
I tbsp	cumin seeds	15 mL
I tbsp	vegetable oil	15 mL
2	onions, finely chopped	2
2	cloves garlic, minced	2
I tbsp	dried oregano leaves	15 mL
I tsp	grated lime zest	5 mL
I tsp	salt	5 mL
½ tsp	cracked black peppercorns	2 mL
I	can (14 to 19 oz/398 to 540 mL) pinto beans, drained and rinsed, or I cup (250 mL) dried pinto beans, soaked, cooked and drained (see Basic Beans, page 100)	I
I	can (28 oz/796 mL) tomatoes, including juice	I
6 cups	vegetable stock	1.5 L
I	can (4.5 oz/127 mL) mild green chilies, drained	I
2 cups	corn kernels, thawed if frozen	500 mL
3	tortillas, preferably corn, cut into 1-inch (2.5 cm) strips	3
	Vegetable oil	
I to 2	avocados, cut into ½-inch (1 cm) cubes	I to 2
	Finely chopped red onion	
	Sour cream (optional)	
	Finely chopped cilantro	

1. In a heatproof bowl, soak chili pepper in boiling water for 30 minutes. Drain and discard stem and soaking water. Set aside.

2. In a dry skillet, over medium heat, toast cumin seeds until they release their aroma and just begin to turn brown. Transfer to a mortar or a spice grinder and grind coarsely. Set aside.

Make ahead

This soup can be partially prepared the night before it is cooked. Complete Steps 1 through 4. Cover and refrigerate overnight. The next morning, continue cooking as directed.

3. In same skillet, heat oil over medium heat. Add onions to pan and cook, stirring, until softened. Add garlic, reserved cumin, oregano, lime zest, salt, peppercorns and reserved New Mexico chili and cook, stirring, for 1 minute. Transfer mixture to a food processor along with beans and 1 cup (250 mL) tomato liquid and process until smooth.

4. Transfer to slow cooker stoneware. If you prefer a smooth soup, add remaining tomatoes to food processor and process until smooth; otherwise, chop coarsely before adding to slow cooker stoneware.

5. Add vegetable stock. Cover and cook on **Low** for 8 to 10 hours or on **High** for 3 to 4 hours, until mixture is bubbling and flavors are combined. Stir in mild green chilies and corn. Cover and cook on **High** for 15 to 20 minutes, until corn is tender.

6. Meanwhile, preheat oven to 400°F (200°C). Brush tortilla strips with oil, place on baking sheet and bake for 4 minutes per side, until crisp and golden.

7. When ready to serve, ladle soup into bowls, lay tortilla strips across surface and top with chopped avocado, red onion, sour cream, if using, and cilantro.

Savory Cheddar Cheese Soup

SERVES 4 TO 6 AS A LIGHT MEAL OR 8 AS A STARTER

• • • • •

This hearty meal-in-a-bowl, which is deliciously rich, is a real show-stopper. It makes a great weeknight dinner with salad or doubles as a starter to a traditional meal. My family likes to scoop up the vegetables on thick slices of country bread, but if you're serving this to guests, puréeing the mixture in a food processor before adding the cream and cheese produces a more polished result.

• • • • •

Tip

Be sure to use Enhanced Vegetable Stock in this soup to ensure the most flavorful result.

• • • • •

Make ahead

This dish can be assembled the night before it is cooked but without adding the cream, cheese and hot pepper sauce, if using. Complete Step 1 and refrigerate overnight. The next day, continue cooking as directed in Step 2.

1 tbsp	butter	15 mL
2	leeks, white part with just a bit of green, cleaned and finely chopped (See Tip, page 41)	2
2	medium carrots, finely chopped	2
3	stalks celery, peeled and finely chopped	3
1 tsp	dry mustard	5 mL
1/2 tsp	salt	2 mL
1/2 tsp	freshly ground black pepper	2 mL
2 tbsp	all-purpose flour	25 mL
5 cups	Enhanced Vegetable Stock (see recipe, page 38)	1.25 L
1 tbsp	tomato paste	15 mL
1	bay leaf	1
1/2 cup	whipping (35%) cream	125 mL
3 cups	shredded Cheddar cheese	750 mL
	Hot pepper sauce to taste (optional)	

1. In a large skillet, melt butter over medium heat. Add leeks, carrots and celery. Turn heat to low, cover and cook for 10 minutes, until vegetables are softened. Add dry mustard, salt, pepper and flour to pan and cook, stirring, for 1 minute. Add stock, tomato paste and bay leaf and cook until slightly thickened.

2. Transfer mixture to slow cooker stoneware. Cover and cook on **Low** for 8 to 10 hours or on **High** for 4 to 5 hours. Discard bay leaf. If desired, transfer solids plus 1 cup (250 mL) liquid to a food processor and process until smooth, then return mixture to slow cooker.

3. Add cream and cheese, cover and cook on **High** for 15 minutes, until cheese is melted and mixture is bubbling. Ladle into individual serving bowls and pass the hot pepper sauce, if desired.

Casseroles and Stews

Vegetable Cobbler

SERVES 6 TO 8

• • • • •

This delicious one-dish meal is the ultimate comfort food. If you wish to serve a salad, sliced tomatoes tossed in oil and vinegar make a nice accompaniment.

• • • • •

Tips

I have not added salt to the vegetable mixture. There is likely to be enough in the mushroom soup and prepared vegetable stock to season the vegetables. Taste and adjust seasoning before transferring to the slow cooker, bearing in mind that the topping also contains salt.

Ensuring that the vegetable mixture is bubbling before adding the topping helps to keep the cobbler from becoming soggy on the bottom.

Unlike milk or cream, condensed cream soup won't curdle if it is cooked for a long period of time. As a result, it's useful when making slow cooker dishes based on a cream sauce.

1 tbsp	butter	15 mL
3	medium leeks, white part only with just a bit of green, cleaned and thinly sliced (see Tip, page 77)	3
4	stalks celery, peeled and thinly sliced	4
4	carrots, peeled and thinly sliced	4
3	cloves garlic, minced	3
2 tsp	dried thyme leaves	10 mL
1 tsp	cracked black peppercorns	5 mL
1 tbsp	all-purpose flour	15 mL
1	can (10 oz/284 mL) condensed cream of mushroom soup (see Tips, left)	1
1 cup	vegetable stock	250 mL
8 oz	portobello or cremini mushrooms, stems removed and chopped	250 g
½ cup	whipping (35%) cream	125 mL
1 cup	frozen green peas, thawed	250 mL
½ cup	finely chopped dill	125 mL

TOPPING

1½ cups	all-purpose flour	375 mL
1 tbsp	baking powder	15 mL
1 tsp	salt	5 mL
6	green onions, white part only, finely chopped	6
1	egg, beaten	1
½ cup	milk	125 mL

1. In a skillet, melt butter over medium heat. Add leeks, celery and carrots, and cook, stirring, until softened, about 7 minutes. Add garlic, thyme and peppercorns and cook, stirring, for 1 minute. Sprinkle flour over mixture and cook, stirring, for 1 minute. Stir in mushroom soup until mixture is smooth (it will be very thick). Then stir in vegetable stock until smooth. Add mushrooms and stir well. Transfer to slow cooker stoneware.

To prevent accumulated moisture from dripping on the cobbler topping, place two clean tea towels, each folded in half (so you will have four layers) across the top of the stoneware before covering. The towels will absorb the moisture generated during cooking.

• • • • •

Make ahead

This dish can be partially prepared the night before it is cooked. Complete Step 1. The next morning, continue cooking as directed.

2. Cover and cook on **Low** for 8 to 10 hours or on **High** for 4 to 5 hours, until vegetables are tender. If cooking on **Low**, increase heat to **High**. Stir in cream, peas and dill. Taste for seasoning and adjust.

3. Topping: In a bowl, combine flour, baking powder and salt. Stir in green onions. Mix in egg and milk to make a lumpy dough. When vegetable mixture is bubbling, drop batter in dollops over the top. Place tea towels over top of stoneware (See Tip, left). Cover and cook on **High** for 30 to 40 minutes or until a toothpick inserted in center of batter comes out clean.

Vegetable Stroganoff

SERVES 6

• • • • •

This robust stew makes a delicious dinner with a salad and crusty bread. You can also serve it over hot noodles.

• • • • •

Tips

If you're using portobello mushrooms, discard the stem, cut them into quarters and thinly slice. If you're using cremini mushrooms, trim off the tough end of the stem and cut them into quarters. Save the stems for making vegetable stock.

Use only good quality blue cheese such as Maytag or Italian Gorgonzola for this recipe as blue cheese of lesser quality tends to be very harsh. If you are in a hurry, warm the cream and cheese, before adding to the stoneware. Stir in and serve as soon as the cheese melts.

• • • • •

Make ahead

This dish can be partially prepared the night before it is cooked. Complete Steps 1 and 2. Cover and refrigerate. The next morning, continue with Step 3.

I tbsp	butter, divided	15 mL
2	large leeks, white part only, cleaned and thinly sliced (see Tip, page 77)	2
4	stalks celery, peeled and thinly sliced	4
2	cloves garlic, minced	2
I tsp	dried thyme leaves	5 mL
I tsp	cracked black peppercorns	5 mL
I tsp	salt	5 mL
I	can (28 oz/796 mL) tomatoes, including juice, coarsely chopped	I
I cup	vegetable stock	250 mL
I lb	portobello or cremini mushrooms, stems removed and sliced (see Tips, left)	500 g
2 to 3	potatoes, peeled and cut into ½-inch (I cm) cubes	2 to 3
½ cup	whipping (35%) cream	125 mL
3 oz	good quality blue cheese, such as Maytag or Gorgonzola, crumbled, and at room temperature (see Tips, left)	90 g

1. In a skillet, melt butter over medium heat. Add leeks and celery and cook, stirring, until softened, about 5 minutes. Add garlic, thyme, peppercorns and salt, stirring, for 1 minute. Add tomatoes with juice and vegetable stock and bring to a boil.

2. Place mushrooms and potatoes in stoneware. Add contents of pan and stir.

3. Cover and cook on **Low** for 8 to 10 hours or on **High** for 4 to 5 hours, until potatoes are tender. Stir in cream and cheese. Cover and cook on **High** for 15 minutes or until cheese is melted into sauce and mixture is hot and bubbling.

Louisiana Ratatouille

SERVES 6

· · · · · ·

Eggplant, tomato and okra stew is a classic Southern dish, which probably owes its origins to the famous Mediterranean mélange ratatouille. The secret to a successful result, even on top of the stove, is not overcooking the okra, which should be added after the other ingredients have melded.

· · · · · ·

Tip

Okra, a tropical vegetable, has a great flavor but it becomes unpleasantly sticky when overcooked. Choose young okra pods, 2 to 4 inches (5 to 10 cm) long, that don't feel sticky to the touch (if sticky, they are too ripe). Gently scrub the pods and cut off the top and tail. Okra can also be found in the freezer section of the grocery store. Thaw before adding to slow cooker.

· · · · · ·

Make ahead

This dish can be partially prepared the night before it is cooked. Complete Steps 1 and 2. Cover and refrigerate overnight. The next morning, continue with Step 3.

2	medium eggplants, peeled, cut into 2-inch (5 cm) cubes, and sweated and drained of excess moisture (see Tips, page 23)	2
2 tbsp	vegetable oil	25 mL
2	onions, finely chopped	2
4	cloves garlic, minced	4
1 tsp	dried oregano leaves	5 mL
1 tsp	salt	5 mL
1/2 tsp	cracked black peppercorns	2 mL
1	can (28 oz/796 mL) tomatoes, including juice, coarsely chopped	1
2 tbsp	red wine vinegar	25 mL
1 lb	okra, trimmed and cut into 1-inch (2 cm) lengths, about 2 cups (500 mL) (see Tip, left)	500 g
1	green bell pepper, cut into 1/4-inch (0.5 cm) dice	1

1. In a nonstick skillet, heat oil over medium heat. Add eggplant, in batches, and cook, stirring, until lightly browned. Transfer to slow cooker stoneware.

2. Add onions to pan and cook, stirring, until softened. Add garlic, oregano, salt and peppercorns and cook, stirring, for 1 minute. Stir in tomatoes with juice and red wine vinegar and bring to a boil. Transfer to slow cooker stoneware.

3. Cover and cook on **Low** for 8 hours or on **High** for 4 hours, until hot and bubbling. Add okra and green pepper. Cover and cook on **High** for 30 minutes, until okra is tender.

Tofu in Indian-Spiced Tomato Sauce

SERVES 4 TO 6

• • • • •

This robust dish makes a lively and different meal. I like to serve it with fresh green beans and naan, an Indian bread, to soak up the sauce.

• • • • •

Make ahead

This dish can be partially prepared the night before it is cooked. Complete Step 1. Cover and refrigerate overnight. The next morning, continue cooking as directed.

1 tbsp	vegetable oil	15 mL
2	onions, finely chopped	2
2	cloves garlic, minced	2
½ tsp	minced gingerroot	2 mL
1	long green chili pepper, seeded and finely chopped	1
6	whole cloves	6
4	pods white or green cardamom	4
1	cinnamon stick piece, about 2 inches (5 cm)	1
1 tsp	caraway seeds	5 mL
1 tsp	salt	5 mL
½ tsp	cracked black peppercorns	2 mL
1	can (28 oz/796 mL) tomatoes, including juice	1

TOFU

¼ cup	all-purpose flour	50 mL
1 tsp	curry powder	5 mL
¼ tsp	cayenne pepper	1 mL
1 tbsp	vegetable oil	15 mL
8 oz	firm tofu, cut into 1-inch (2.5 cm) squares	250 g

1. In a skillet, heat oil over medium heat. Add onions and cook, stirring, until softened. Add garlic, gingerroot, chili pepper, cloves, cardamom, cinnamon stick, caraway seeds, salt and peppercorns and cook, stirring, for 1 minute. Add tomatoes with juice and bring to a boil. Transfer to slow cooker stoneware.

2. Cover and cook on **Low** for 8 to 10 hours or on **High** for 4 to 5 hours.

3. Tofu: On a plate, mix together flour, curry powder and cayenne. Roll tofu in mixture until lightly coated. Discard excess flour. In a skillet, heat oil over medium-high heat. Add dredged tofu and sauté, stirring, until nicely browned. Spoon tomato mixture into a serving dish. Discard cloves, cardamom and cinnamon stick. Layer tofu on top.

French Onion Soup *page 39* ➤
Overleaf: Red Lentil and Carrot Soup with Coconut *page 50*

Wild Rice with Mushrooms and Apricots

SERVES 4

• • • • •

This combination of wild and brown rice with dried apricots makes a tasty weeknight meal. Be sure to serve it with a good chutney alongside — tomato or spicy mango work very well. A grated carrot salad is a nice accompaniment.

• • • • •

Tips

You can purchase wild and brown rice mixtures in many supermarkets, or you can make your own by combining ½ cup (125 mL) of each.

Accumulated moisture affects the consistency of the rice. The folded tea towels will absorb the moisture generated during cooking.

1 tbsp	vegetable oil	15 mL
1	onion, chopped	1
4	stalks celery, diced	4
2	cloves garlic, minced	2
1 cup	wild rice and brown rice mixture, rinsed (see Tips, left)	250 mL
8 oz	portobello or cremini mushrooms stems removed and diced	250 g
	Salt and freshly ground black pepper, to taste	
2 cups	vegetable stock	500 mL
1 tbsp	balsamic vinegar	15 mL
¼ cup	chopped dried apricots	50 mL
	Chutney	

1. In a skillet, heat oil over medium heat. Add onion and celery and cook, stirring, until softened, about 5 minutes. Add garlic and rice and stir until coated. Stir in mushrooms and salt and pepper. Add stock and balsamic vinegar and bring to a boil. Transfer to prepared slow cooker. Stir in apricots.

2. Place two clean tea towels, each folded in half (so you will have four layers), over top of slow cooker stoneware (see Tips, left). Cover and cook on **Low** for 7 to 8 hours or on **High** for 4 hours, until rice is tender and liquid has been absorbed. Serve hot accompanied by your favorite fruit chutney.

Vegetable Curry with Pepper and Cilantro Tadka

SERVES 6

• • • • •

This delicious vegetable curry is a favorite weekday main course. Tadka, a fried garnish often used in Indian cooking, is traditionally a mixture of spices cooked in ghee, a type of clarified butter. It is usually served over a large bowl of dal made from dried beans or lentils. I like the spicy finish the tadka adds to this mellow stew, but I prefer to pass it in a small bowl, allowing people to season to taste.

1 tbsp	vegetable oil	15 mL
2	large leeks, white part only, cleaned and thinly sliced (see Tip, page 77)	2
6	stalks celery, peeled and thinly sliced	6
6	carrots, peeled and thinly sliced	6
4	cloves garlic, minced	4
1 tbsp	minced gingerroot	15 mL
1 tbsp	curry powder	15 mL
1	chili pepper, finely chopped	1
1	can (28 oz/796 mL) tomatoes, including juice, coarsely chopped (see Tip, page 46)	1
2	potatoes, peeled and shredded	2
2 cups	lentils, washed and picked over	500 mL
3 cups	vegetable stock	750 mL
2 cups	green beans, cut into 1-inch (2.5 cm) pieces, or green peas, thawed if frozen	500 mL

PEPPER AND CILANTRO TADKA

1 tsp	cumin seeds	5 mL
2 tbsp	ghee, clarified butter or vegetable oil	25 mL
2	green onions, white part only, finely chopped	2
½	chili pepper, finely chopped	½
1	red bell pepper, finely chopped	1
¼ cup	finely chopped cilantro	50 mL
1 tbsp	freshly squeezed lemon juice	15 mL

1. In a skillet, heat oil over medium heat. Add leeks, celery and carrots and stir to combine. Reduce heat to low, cover and cook until vegetables are soft, about 10 minutes.

2. Increase heat to medium. Add garlic, gingerroot, curry powder and chili pepper and cook, stirring, for 1 minute. Stir in tomatoes with juice and bring to a boil.

3. Place potatoes and lentils in slow cooker stoneware. Pour contents of pan over mixture and stir well. Add stock barely to cover, about 3 cups (750 mL).

4. Cover and cook on **Low** for 8 to 10 hours or on **High** for 4 to 5 hours, until vegetables are tender. Add green beans or peas. Cover and cook on **High** until tender, about 15 to 30 minutes.

5. Pepper and Cilantro Tadka: In a skillet, over medium heat, toast cumin seeds just until they begin to turn brown and release their aroma. Remove from heat, grind and set aside. In same skillet, heat ghee, clarified butter or oil. Add green onions, chili pepper, red pepper and cook, stirring, for 1 minute. Remove from heat. Stir in cilantro, lemon juice and reserved cumin seeds. Spoon into a small bowl and serve as a garnish for the curry.

Rigatoni with Fennel and Spicy Peppers

SERVES 4

• • • • •

This combination of tomatoes, pasta and fennel is a real winner. The hot peppers add a nice finish — vary the quantity to accommodate your affinity for heat.

• • • • •

Tip

If you don't like spicy peppers, serve this with roasted red peppers tossed in olive oil.

• • • • •

Make ahead

This dish can be partially prepared the night before it is cooked. Complete Steps 1 and 2. Cover and refrigerate overnight. The next day continue cooking as directed.

• Lightly greased slow cooker stoneware

4 cups	rigatoni	750 mL
I tbsp	vegetable oil	15 mL
2	bulbs fennel, base and leafy stems discarded, bulb cut into thin slices	2
I	onion, finely chopped	I
4	cloves garlic, minced	4
I tsp	fennel seeds (optional)	5 mL
I tsp	salt	5 mL
½ tsp	cracked black peppercorns	2 mL
I	can (28 oz/796 mL) tomatoes, including juice, coarsely chopped	I
½ cup	freshly grated Parmesan cheese (optional)	125 mL

SPICY PEPPERS

1 to 2 tbsp	olive oil	15 to 25 mL
2 to 4	hot yellow banana peppers, finely chopped	2 to 4

1. In a large pot of boiling salted water, cook rigatoni until barely tender, about 7 minutes once water returns to a boil. Drain and set aside.

2. In a skillet, heat oil over medium heat. Add fennel and onion and cook, stirring, until fennel is softened, about 6 minutes. Add garlic, fennel seeds, if using, salt and peppercorns and cook, stirring, for 1 minute. Add tomatoes with juice and bring to a boil. Transfer to slow cooker stoneware. Add cooked rigatoni and stir to combine. Sprinkle Parmesan, if using, evenly over rigatoni.

3. Cover and cook on **Low** for 8 hours or **High** for 4 hours, until hot and bubbling.

4. Spicy Peppers: In a small skillet, heat olive oil over medium heat. Add peppers and cook until softened, about 4 minutes. Transfer to a small bowl and pass at the table.

Cannelloni with Tomato Eggplant Sauce

SERVES 8

• • • • •

Here's a great recipe for cannelloni that is remarkably easy to make. Oven-ready pasta is filled with ricotta and baby spinach and bathed in a tomato eggplant sauce. Add some crusty bread and a salad of roasted peppers or crisp greens for a terrific meal.

• • • • •

Tip

Be sure to use oven-ready cannelloni or manicotti in this recipe. It is a great time saver and it cooks to perfection in the slow cooker.

• • • • •

Make ahead

This dish can be prepared the night before it is cooked. Let tomato sauce cool before pouring over cannelloni. Refrigerate overnight in slow cooker stoneware and cook as directed.

SAUCE

1	medium eggplant, peeled, cut into 2-inch (5 cm) cubes, and sweated and drained of excess moisture (see Tips, page 23)	1
2 tbsp	olive oil	25 mL
2	cloves garlic, minced	2
¼ tsp	freshly ground black pepper	1 mL
3 cups	tomato sauce	750 mL

FILLING

2 cups	ricotta cheese	500 mL
½ cup	freshly grated Parmesan cheese	125 mL
1½ cups	chopped baby spinach	375 mL
1 tsp	freshly grated nutmeg	5 mL
1	egg, beaten	1
¼ tsp	salt	1 mL
¼ tsp	freshly ground black pepper	1 mL
24	oven-ready cannelloni shells	24

1. **Sauce:** In a nonstick skillet, heat oil over medium heat. Add eggplant, in batches, and cook until it begins to brown. Add garlic and black pepper and cook, stirring, for 1 minute. Add tomato sauce, stir well and bring to a boil. Remove from heat and set aside.

2. **Filling:** In a bowl, combine ricotta, Parmesan, spinach, nutmeg, egg, salt and pepper. Using your fingers, fill pasta shells with mixture and place filled shells side by side in slow cooker stoneware, then on top of each other when bottom layer is complete. Pour sauce over shells. Cover and cook on **Low** for 8 hours or on **High** for 4 hours, until hot and bubbling.

Cheesy Rice and Mushroom Casserole with Spinach

SERVES 6

• • • • •

Your family will love this tasty one-pot dinner. Add a green, shredded carrot or sliced tomato salad, if you prefer, but if you're pressed for time, just serve hot crusty rolls. This is an ideal meal for those evenings when everyone is coming and going at different times, as it can be kept warm in the slow cooker and people can help themselves.

• • • • •

Tip

Accumulated moisture affects the consistency of the rice. The folded tea towels will absorb the moisture generated during cooking.

• • • • •

Make ahead

This dish can be partially prepared the night before it is cooked. Cut mushrooms. Cover and refrigerate. Complete Steps 1 and 2. Cover and refrigerate overnight. The next day, continue cooking as directed in Step 3.

I tbsp	cumin seeds	15 mL
I tbsp	vegetable oil	15 mL
2	onions, finely chopped	2
4	stalks celery, peeled and thinly sliced	4
2	cloves garlic, minced	2
I tbsp	minced gingerroot	15 mL
I tsp	salt	5 mL
I tsp	crushed black peppercorns	5 mL
2 cups	long-grain brown rice	500 mL
¼ cup	oil-packed sun-dried tomatoes, finely chopped	50 mL
I	can (28 oz/796 mL) tomatoes, including juice, coarsely chopped (see Tip, page 46)	I
3 cups	vegetable stock	750 mL
2	large portobello mushrooms, stems removed, cut into ½-inch (I cm) cubes	2
8 oz	fresh spinach leaves or I package (10 oz/300 g) spinach, washed, stems removed and chopped	250 g
2 cups	shredded Cheddar cheese	500 mL

1. In a dry skillet, over medium heat, toast cumin seeds until they release their aroma and just begin to turn brown. Transfer to a mortar or a spice grinder and grind coarsely. Set aside.

2. In a skillet, heat oil over medium heat. Add onions and celery and cook, stirring, until softened, about 5 minutes. Add garlic, gingerroot, reserved cumin, salt, peppercorns and rice and cook, stirring, for 1 minute. Add sun-dried tomatoes, tomatoes with juice and vegetable stock and bring to a boil.

3. Place mushrooms in slow cooker stoneware. Pour rice mixture over mushrooms and stir to combine.

4. Place two clean tea towels, each folded in half (so you will have four layers), across the top of slow cooker stoneware. Cover and cook on **Low** for 7 to 8 hours or **High** for 4 hours, until rice is tender and has absorbed the liquid. Remove tea towels. Stir in spinach and sprinkle cheese over top of mixture. Cover and cook on **High** for 20 to 25 minutes, until spinach is cooked and cheese is melted. Serve piping hot.

Mushroom and Artichoke Lasagna

SERVES 8

· · · · ·

I love the unusual
combination of flavors in
this lasagna, which reminds
me of a Provençal gratin.
In addition to adding flavor
and color, the baby spinach
is a great time saver as it
doesn't require pre-cooking.

· · · · ·

Tips

Unlike many recipes for
lasagna, this one is not terribly
saucy. As a result, the noodles
on the top layer tend to dry
out. Leave a small amount of
the cooking liquid from the
mushroom mixture behind
in the pan, after adding to the
slow cooker. Pour that over
the top layer of noodles,
particularly around the edges,
where they are most likely
to dry out.

Use white or cremini
mushrooms or a combination
of the two in this recipe.

· · · · ·

Make ahead

This dish can be prepared
the night before it is cooked.
Refrigerate overnight in
slow cooker stoneware and
cook as directed.

· Large (minimum 5 quart) oval slow cooker, greased

2 tbsp	butter	25 mL
1	onion, finely chopped	1
1 lb	mushrooms, stems removed and sliced	500 g
4	cloves garlic, minced	4
3½ cups	quartered artichoke hearts, packed in water, drained, or thawed if frozen	875 mL
¾ cup	dry white wine or vegetable stock	175 mL
12	oven-ready lasagna noodles	12
2½ cups	ricotta cheese	625 mL
2 cups	baby spinach	500 mL
2½ cups	shredded mozzarella cheese	625 mL
½ cup	freshly grated Parmesan cheese	125 mL

1. In a skillet, melt butter over medium heat. Add
onion and cook until softened. Add mushrooms and
garlic and cook, stirring, just until mushrooms begin
to release their liquid. Stir in artichokes and wine and
bring to a boil. Cook, stirring, for 1 or 2 minutes, until
liquid reduces slightly. Set aside.

2. Cover bottom of slow cooker stoneware with
4 noodles, breaking to fit where necessary. Spread
with half of the ricotta, half of the mushroom mixture,
half of the spinach, one-third each of the mozzarella and
Parmesan. Repeat. Arrange final layer of noodles over
cheeses. Pour any liquid remaining from mushroom
mixture over noodles (see Tips, left) and sprinkle with
remaining Parmesan and mozzarella. Cover and cook
on **Low** for 6 to 8 hours or on **High** for 3 to 4 hours,
until hot and bubbling.

Tomato Mushroom Lasagna

SERVES 6 TO 8

• • • • •

Lasagna is a family favorite — in our house at least. Serve this with a tossed salad for a delicious and nutritious meal.

• • • • •

Tip

Oven-ready noodles are a great time saver when preparing lasagna. Happily, the moisture generated in the slow cooker is a benefit when using this product, which in my experience works better in the slow cooker than in the oven, where the noodles can become a bit chewy.

• • • • •

Make ahead

This dish can be prepared the night before it is cooked. Refrigerate overnight in slow cooker stoneware and cook as directed.

• Large (minimum 5 quart) oval slow cooker, greased

I tbsp	vegetable oil	15 mL
4	large portobello mushrooms, cut in half and thinly sliced	4
2	cloves garlic, minced	2
I tsp	salt	5 mL
½ tsp	cracked black peppercorns	2 mL
I tbsp	freshly squeezed lemon juice	15 mL
3 cups	tomato sauce	750 mL
12	oven-ready lasagna noodles	12
2 cups	ricotta cheese	500 mL
½ cup	freshly grated Parmesan cheese	250 mL
2 cups	shredded mozzarella cheese	500 mL

1. In a skillet, heat oil over medium heat. Add mushrooms and cook, stirring, just until they begin to release their liquid. Add garlic and cook, stirring, for 1 minute. Remove from heat and stir in salt, peppercorns and lemon juice. Set aside.

2. Spread one-quarter of tomato sauce over bottom of prepared slow cooker. Cover with 4 noodles, breaking to fit where necessary. Spread with half of the ricotta, half of the mushroom mixture, one-third each of the Parmesan and mozzarella. Repeat. Arrange final layer of noodles over cheeses. Pour remaining sauce over top and sprinkle with remaining Parmesan and mozzarella. Cover and cook on **Low** for 6 to 8 hours or on **High** for 3 to 4 hours, until hot and bubbling.

Pozole

SERVES 8

• • • • •

Pozole, a hearty stew made from hominy and Mexican in origin, is distinguished by its toppings. I like to serve this with shredded lettuce, chopped red or green onion, finely chopped cilantro and avocado slices. Sliced radishes are a nice addition in season. In Mexico, shredded cabbage, fried tortillas or toasted pumpkin seeds are also used as garnishes and hot sauce may be added as a finish. Serve with lime wedges so people can season with citrus, to taste. This makes a big batch, but leftovers reheat well.

• • • • •

Tip

If you like the flavor of epazote, a Mexican herb, add about 1 tsp (5 mL) dried epazote along with the oregano or stir about 1 tbsp (15 mL) finely chopped fresh epazote into the pozole before garnishing. These quantities are conservative, but epazote is very pungent. You can always add more the next time.

2	dried ancho chili peppers	2
2 cups	boiling water	500 mL
2 tbsp	pumpkin seeds	25 mL
1 tbsp	cumin seeds	15 mL
1 tbsp	vegetable oil	15 mL
2	onions finely chopped	2
4	cloves garlic, minced	4
1 tbsp	dried oregano, preferably Mexican	15 mL
1 tsp	salt	5 mL
1/2 tsp	cracked black peppercorns	2 mL
1	can (28 oz/796 mL) tomatoes, including juice, coarsely chopped	1
1 cup	vegetable stock	250 mL
2	cans (each 29 oz/824 mL) hominy, drained and rinsed	2
	Zest and juice of 1 lime	
1	red bell pepper, diced	1
1	green bell pepper, diced	1
	Shredded lettuce	
	Finely chopped red or green onion	
	Avocado slices	
	Finely chopped cilantro	
	Lime wedges	

1. In a heatproof bowl, soak dried chilies in boiling water for 30 minutes. Drain and discard soaking liquid and stems. Set aside.

2. In a dry skillet, over medium-high heat, toast pumpkin and cumin seeds, until pumpkin seeds are popping and cumin has released its aroma. Transfer to a small bowl and set aside.

Make ahead

This dish can be partially prepared the night before it is served. Complete Steps 1 and 2. The next morning, continue cooking as directed in Step 3.

3. In same skillet, heat oil over medium heat. Add onions and cook, stirring, until softened, about 3 minutes. Add garlic, oregano, salt and peppercorns and cook, stirring, for 1 minute. Transfer contents of pan to a food processor. Add tomatoes with juice, reserved ancho peppers, pumpkin and cumin seeds and process until smooth. In slow cooker stoneware, combine vegetable broth, tomato mixture and hominy.

4. Cover and cook on **Low** for 6 to 8 hours or on **High** for 3 to 4 hours, until mixture is bubbling. Stir in lime zest and juice and bell peppers. Cover and cook on **High** for 15 minutes, until peppers are tender. Ladle into bowls and garnish, as desired.

Rigatoni and Cheese

SERVES 4

● ● ● ● ●

Here's a comfort food favorite that works well in the slow cooker when made with rigatoni rather than the traditional macaroni. Serve with a tossed salad and crusty bread for a tasty family meal.

● ● ● ● ●

Tip

Placing tea towels over top of the slow cooker prevents accumulated moisture from dripping on the topping.

● ● ● ● ●

Make ahead

This dish can be partially assembled the night before it is cooked. Complete Steps 1, 2 and 3. Cover and refrigerate overnight. The next morning, continue with Step 4.

● Lightly greased slow cooker stoneware

3 cups	rigatoni, cooked until barely tender	750 mL
I	can (28 oz/796 mL) tomatoes, drained, reserving I cup (250 mL) liquid	I
I	can (10 oz/284 mL) condensed cream of mushroom soup	I
I tsp	dried oregano leaves	5 mL
I tsp	salt	5 mL
½ tsp	cracked black peppercorns	2 mL
2½ cups	shredded Cheddar cheese	625 mL
½ cup	freshly grated Parmesan cheese	125 mL
½ cup	fine fresh bread crumbs	125 mL
2 tbsp	melted butter	25 mL

1. In a large pot of boiling salted water, cook rigatoni until barely tender, about 7 minutes once water returns to a boil. Drain and set aside.

2. In a food processor, combine tomatoes plus reserved liquid, soup, oregano, salt and peppercorns. Pulse three or four times, until tomatoes are coarsely chopped and mixture is combined.

3. In slow cooker stoneware, combine rigatoni, Cheddar cheese and tomato mixture.

4. In a bowl, mix together Parmesan cheese and bread crumbs. Sprinkle evenly over rigatoni. Drizzle with butter. Place two clean tea towels, each folded in half (so you will have four layers), across the top of the slow cooker stoneware. Cover and cook on **Low** for 8 hours or on **High** for 4 hours, until hot and bubbling.

Leek and Barley Risotto

SERVES 4

• • • • •

This tasty "risotto," makes an interesting centerpiece of a light meal, served with a salad and hot, crusty bread. In season, add some steamed yellow waxed beans, tossed with butter or butter substitute, lemon juice and finely chopped fresh dill.

• • • • •

Tip

To clean leeks: Fill sink full of lukewarm water. Split leeks in half lengthwise and submerge in water, swishing them around to remove all traces of dirt. Transfer to a colander and rinse under cold water.

• • • • •

Make ahead

This dish can be partially prepared the night before it is cooked. Complete Step 1. Cover and refrigerate overnight. The next morning, continue with Step 2.

1 tbsp	vegetable oil	15 mL
3	leeks, white part only, cleaned and thinly sliced (see Tip, left)	3
1 tsp	salt	5 mL
½ tsp	cracked black peppercorns	2 mL
2 cups	pearl barley, rinsed	500 mL
1	can (28 oz/796 mL) tomatoes, including juice, coarsely chopped	1
3 cups	vegetable stock or water	750 mL
	Freshly grated Parmesan cheese (optional)	

1. In a skillet, heat oil over medium heat. Add leeks and cook, stirring, until softened. Add salt, peppercorns and barley and cook, stirring, for 1 minute. Add tomatoes with juice and stock and bring to a boil. Transfer to slow cooker stoneware.

2. Cover and cook on **Low** for 8 hours or on **High** for 4 hours. Stir in Parmesan, if using, and serve piping hot.

Sweet Potato Barley Risotto

SERVES 4

• • • • •

Serve this delicious and unusual "risotto" with a tossed green salad and whole grain rolls for a tasty and nutritious meal.

• • • • •

Make ahead

This dish can be partially prepared the night before it is cooked. Complete Steps 1 and 2. Cover and refrigerate overnight. The next morning, continue with Step 3.

1 tbsp	vegetable oil	15 mL
2	onions, finely chopped	2
2	cloves garlic, minced	2
1/2 tsp	dried rosemary leaves	2 mL
1 1/2 cups	pearl barley, rinsed	375 mL
3 cups	vegetable stock	750 mL
2	sweet potato, peeled and cut into 1/4-inch (0.5 cm) cubes	2
	Freshly grated Parmesan cheese (optional)	

1. In a skillet, heat oil over medium heat. Add onions and cook, stirring, until softened. Add garlic and rosemary and cook, stirring, for 1 minute. Stir in barley until well coated with mixture. Add stock and bring to a boil.

2. Place sweet potatoes in slow cooker stoneware. Cover with barley mixture and stir to combine.

3. Cover and cook on **Low** for 8 hours or on **High** for 4 hours, until barley and sweet potato are tender. Stir in Parmesan, if using, and serve immediately.

Eggplant and Potato Curry

SERVES 6

• • • • •

This delicious curry is a great centerpiece for a festive meal. Make an effort to find tomato chutney, which can be difficult to locate, as it is the perfect finish to this ambrosial stew.

• • • • •

Tip

If you can't find tomato chutney, use tomato-based chili sauce instead.

• • • • •

Make ahead

This dish can be assembled the night before is it cooked. Complete Steps 1 and 2. Cover and refrigerate overnight. The next morning, continue with Step 3.

2	medium eggplants, peeled, cut into 2-inch (5 cm) cubes, and sweated and drained of excess moisture (see Tips, 23)	2
2 tbsp	vegetable oil, divided (approx.)	25 mL
2	potatoes, peeled and diced	2
2	onions, finely chopped	2
2	cloves garlic, minced	2
1 tsp	minced gingerroot	5 mL
1	long red chili pepper, finely chopped (optional)	1
2 tsp	curry powder	10 mL
1/2 tsp	salt	2 mL
1/2 tsp	cracked black peppercorns	2 mL
1 tbsp	tomato paste	15 mL
1 cup	vegetable stock	250 mL
	Tomato chutney (see Tip, left)	

1. In a nonstick skillet, heat 1 tbsp (15 mL) oil over medium heat. Add sweated eggplant, in batches, and cook until browned. Transfer to slow cooker stoneware. Add potatoes to stoneware and return pan to element.

2. Add onions to pan, adding remaining oil if necessary, and cook, stirring, until softened, about 3 minutes. Add garlic, gingerroot, chili, if using, curry powder, salt and peppercorns and cook, stirring, for 1 minute. Stir in tomato paste and vegetable stock. Pour mixture over vegetables in stoneware.

3. Cover and cook on **Low** for 8 hours or on **High** for 4 hours, until hot and bubbling. Stir in tomato chutney to taste, or pass at the table.

Green Beans 'n' Barley

SERVES 4

• • • • •

North Americans are
accustomed to eating
green beans crisply cooked
in stir-fries or as a side dish.
But in some Europeans
countries it is common to
find them more thoroughly
cooked in stew-like dishes.
Here's an update of a classic
1960s recipe featuring
cream of mushroom soup.
I've added barley to make
it a substantial main course.
Add a tossed green salad to
complete the meal.

• • • • •

Tip

For convenience, use frozen
sliced green beans. Don't
thaw them. Increase the
cooking time to 8 hours on
Low or 4 hours on **High**.

• • • • •

Make ahead

This dish can be completely
assembled the night before it
is cooked unless you are using
frozen green beans and wish
to extend the cooking time.
If so, complete Step 1 without
adding the beans. The next
morning add the frozen
beans, cover and cook for
8 hours on **Low** or 4 hours
on **High**.

1	can (10 oz/284 mL) condensed cream of mushroom soup	1
½ cup	finely chopped green onions	125 mL
1 tbsp	minced garlic	15 mL
½ tsp	dried tarragon	2 mL
½ tsp	cracked black peppercorns	2 mL
2 tbsp	soy sauce	25 mL
2 cups	vegetable stock	500 mL
2 cups	green beans, cut into ½-inch (1 cm) lengths	500 mL
1 cup	pearl barley, rinsed	250 mL
2 tbsp	toasted pine nuts (optional)	25 mL

1. In slow cooker stoneware, combine soup, green onions,
garlic, tarragon, peppercorns and soy sauce. Beat until
smooth. Gradually add vegetable stock, beating until
mixture is smooth. Stir in green beans and barley.

2. Cover and cook on **Low** for 6 hours or on **High** for
3 hours, until hot and bubbling. Sprinkle with toasted
pine nuts, if using.

Fennel, Tomato and Potato Ragout

SERVES 4

• • • • •

This tasty vegetable stew is particularly delicious topped with *rouille*, a seasoned mayonnaise. *Rouille* is very easy to make using prepared mayonnaise, but if you don't have the time or inclination to prepare it, finish this dish with shaved Parmesan or even a dollop of prepared basil pesto. Serve with hot rice or a crusty country loaf. Add a tossed green salad to complete the meal.

• • • • •

Tips

Instead of *rouille*, garnish the ragout with slices of shaved Parmesan.

Or stir in prepared basil pesto, to taste.

1/8 tsp	saffron	0.5 mL
1 tbsp	vegetable oil	15 mL
2	onions, finely chopped	2
4	cloves garlic, minced	4
2 tsp	dried Italian seasoning	10 mL
1	can (28 oz/796 mL) diced tomatoes, including juice	1
1 cup	vegetable stock	250 mL
3	potatoes, peeled and cut into 1/2-inch (1 cm) cubes	3
2	fennel bulbs, base and leafy stems discarded, coarsely chopped	2
1/2 cup	pitted black olives, coarsely chopped	125 mL

EASY ROUILLE (OPTIONAL)

1/2 cup	mayonnaise	125 mL
2	cloves garlic, grated or put through a press	2
1/8 tsp	saffron threads	0.5 mL
1/8 tsp	cayenne pepper	0.5 mL

1. Crumble saffron between your thumb and fingers into a small bowl. Add 1 tbsp (15 mL) boiling water and stir well. Set aside.

2. In a skillet, heat oil over medium heat. Add onions and cook, stirring, until softened, about 3 minutes. Add garlic and Italian seasoning and cook, stirring, for 1 minute. Add saffron water, tomatoes with juice and vegetable stock and bring to a boil.

3. Spread potatoes evenly over the bottom of slow cooker stoneware. Add fennel. Pour contents of skillet over vegetables.

4. Cover and cook on **Low** for 8 hours or on **High** for 4 hours, until potatoes are tender. Stir in olives and serve topped with a spoonful of *rouille*, if using.

5. *Rouille* (optional): In a small bowl, combine mayonnaise, garlic, saffron and cayenne. Mix until thoroughly blended.

Celery Brown Betty

SERVES 6 TO 8

· · · · ·

If your taste buds have grown tired of the same old thing, this recipe is a bit different and easy to make. The hint of caraway complements the celery and adds intriguing flavor to the sauce. I like to serve this over garlic mashed potatoes, with a salad of sliced tomatoes on the side. It reheats well, so don't worry about leftovers.

· · · · ·

Tips

Crush caraway seeds in a mortar with a pestle or on a cutting board, using the bottom of a measuring cup.

The folded tea towels prevent accumulated moisture from dripping on the topping.

· · · · ·

Make ahead

This dish can be assembled the night before it is cooked but without adding the topping. Complete Step 1. Cover and refrigerate over night. The next morning, continue with Step 2.

I	can (10 oz/284 mL) cream of celery soup	I
2 tsp	caraway seeds, coarsely crushed (see Tips, left)	10 mL
½ tsp	cracked black peppercorns	2 mL
I cup	vegetable stock	250 mL
2	bunches celery, thinly sliced, plus leaves finely chopped and set aside	2
2	red onions, thinly sliced	2
I cup	dry bread crumbs	250 mL
¼ cup	freshly grated Parmesan cheese	125 mL
2 tbsp	melted butter	25 mL
I tbsp	grainy mustard	15 mL
¼ tsp	salt	I mL

1. In slow cooker stoneware, combine soup, caraway seeds and peppercorns. Stir to blend. Gradually add vegetable stock, beating to eliminate any lumps that might form. Stir in celery and red onions.

2. In a bowl, combine bread crumbs, Parmesan cheese, butter, mustard and salt. Stir until blended. Spread mixture evenly over contents of slow cooker.

3. Place two clean tea towels, each folded in half (so you will have four layers) across the top of the stoneware. Cover and cook on **Low** for 6 to 8 hours or on **High** for 3 to 4 hours, until hot and bubbling.

Potatoes with Creamy Corn Topping

SERVES 6 TO 8

• • • • •

This dish reminds me of scalloped potatoes, a childhood favorite, dressed up to become a main course. It's much lighter and more nutritious than that old favorite and has an abundance of interesting flavors. Add a green salad or crisp green beans, sprinkled with toasted sesame seeds to complete the meal.

• • • • •

Make ahead

This dish can be partially prepared before it is cooked. Complete Steps 1 through 4. Cover and refrigerate corn mixture and stoneware separately. The next morning continue cooking as directed in Step 5.

• Greased slow cooker stoneware

4 cups	corn kernels, thawed if frozen	1 L
½ cup	evaporated milk	125 mL
1 tbsp	butter	15 mL
½ tsp	freshly grated nutmeg	2 mL
	Freshly ground black pepper, to taste	
1 cup	shredded mozzarella	250 mL
1	can (28 oz/796 mL) tomatoes, including juice	1
½ cup	loosely packed parsley leaves	125 mL
1 tsp	salt	5 mL
4	medium potatoes, thinly sliced, preferably with a mandoline	4
1	red onion, halved and thinly sliced on the vertical	1

1. In a food processor, combine corn and evaporated milk. Process until combined, but corn is still a little chunky.

2. In a skillet, melt butter over medium–low heat. Add corn mixture and cook until thickened, about 5 minutes. Add nutmeg, pepper and mozzarella and stir until cheese is melted. Set aside.

3. Rinse out food processor work bowl. Add tomatoes with juice, parsley and salt and process until smooth.

4. Spread potatoes evenly over bottom of prepared slow cooker stoneware. Spread red onion over top and cover with tomato mixture.

5. Spread corn mixture evenly over top of tomato mixture. Cover and cook on **Low** for 8 hours or **High** for 4 hours, until potatoes are tender and mixture is hot and bubbling.

Leek, Potato and Mushroom Gratin

SERVES 4

• • • • •

Serve this simple gratin with sliced tomatoes in vinaigrette or roasted red peppers tossed in extra virgin olive oil for a tasty meal.

• • • • •

Make ahead

This dish can be partially assembled the night before it is cooked. Complete Steps 1 and 2. Cover and refrigerate overnight. The next morning, continue cooking as directed.

• Greased slow cooker stoneware

2 tbsp	butter, divided	25 mL
8 oz	shiitake mushrooms, stems removed, thinly sliced	250 g
2	medium potatoes, peeled and thinly sliced	2
3	leeks, white part only, cleaned and thinly sliced (see Tip, page 77)	3
I tbsp	minced garlic	15 mL
I tsp	dried thyme leaves	5 mL
I tsp	salt	5 mL
	Freshly ground black pepper, to taste	
I tbsp	all-purpose flour	15 mL
I½ cups	vegetable stock	375 mL

TOPPING

I cup	bread crumbs	250 mL
½ cup	freshly grated Parmesan cheese (optional)	125 mL
I tsp	paprika	5 mL
¼ tsp	salt	I mL
	Freshly ground black pepper, to taste	
2 tbsp	melted butter	25 mL

1. In a skillet, melt 1 tbsp (15 mL) butter over medium heat. Add mushrooms and cook, stirring just until they begin to release their liquid. Remove from heat. Spread potatoes in layers evenly over bottom of prepared slow cooker. Spread mushrooms evenly over top of potatoes.

2. Return skillet to element. Add remaining butter and leeks and cook, stirring, until leeks are softened, about 4 minutes. Add garlic, thyme, salt and pepper and cook, stirring, for 1 minute. Add flour and cook, stirring, for 1 minute. Add vegetable stock and cook, stirring, until mixture thickens, about 3 minutes. Pour over contents of stoneware.

3. Cover and cook on **Low** for 8 hours or on **High** for 4 hours, until potatoes are tender.

4. Topping: In a bowl, combine bread crumbs, Parmesan, if using, paprika, salt and pepper. Mix well. Add butter and stir to blend. Spread mixture evenly over leeks. Cover, leaving lid slightly ajar to prevent accumulated moisture from dripping on the topping, and cook on **High** for 30 minutes, until cheese is melted and mixture is hot and bubbling.

Variation

Creamy Leek, Potato and Mushroom Gratin

For a creamier version of this gratin, bring ½ to 1 cup (125 to 250 mL) of whipping (35 %) cream to a boil on the stovetop or in the microwave. Pour over the cooked vegetables just before adding the topping. Proceed with Step 4.

VEGAN FRIENDLY
Sweet Potatoes and Carrots with Chickpea Topping

SERVES 4

• • • • •

This tasty and nutritious combination of sweet potatoes, carrots and pineapple, finished with a chickpea topping makes a delightfully different main course. Refrigerate any leftovers and transform them into an interesting side dish. Simply purée in a food processor fitted with a metal blade, then reheat in the microwave or over low heat on the stovetop.

• • • • •

Make ahead

This dish can be partially prepared the night before it is cooked. Complete Steps 1 and 2. Cover and refrigerate overnight. The next morning, continue with Step 3.

• Greased slow cooker stoneware

2	sweet potatoes, peeled and cut into ½-inch (1 cm) cubes	2
6	carrots, peeled and thinly sliced	6
1	can (14 oz/398 mL) crushed pineapple, drained, ¼ cup (50 mL) syrup set aside	1
2 tbsp	packed brown sugar	25 mL

TOPPING

1	can (14 to 19 oz/398 to 540 mL) chickpeas, drained and rinsed, or 2 cups (500 mL) cooked chickpeas, drained and rinsed	1
1 tbsp	minced garlic	15 mL
½ cup	vegetable stock	125 mL
	Salt and freshly ground pepper, to taste	

1. In prepared stoneware, combine sweet potato, carrots and pineapple. In a small bowl, combine brown sugar and reserved pineapple juice. Add to stoneware and stir to blend.

2. Topping: In a food processor, fitted with a metal blade, process chickpeas, garlic and vegetable broth until mixture is well combined, but chickpeas are still a little chunky. Season with salt and pepper. Spread mixture evenly over sweet potato mixture.

3. Cover and cook on **Low** for 8 hours or on **High** for 4 hours until vegetables are tender.

Beet Curry with Sweet Green Peas

SERVES 4 TO 6

• • • • •

The addition of tomato chutney transforms this simple curry into a delicious treat. Be sure to buy a flavorful version of this versatile condiment as it makes all the difference to the taste of this dish. Add the chilies if you prefer a spicier version. Serve over fluffy white rice or with warm Indian bread such as naan.

• • • • •

Make ahead

This dish can be partially prepared the night before it is cooked. Complete Steps 1 and 2. Cover and refrigerate overnight. The next morning, continue with Step 3.

1 tbsp	cumin seeds	15 mL
1 tbsp	vegetable oil	15 mL
2	onions, finely chopped	2
4	cloves garlic, finely chopped	4
1 tsp	salt	5 mL
½ tsp	cracked black peppercorns	2 mL
2 cups	vegetable stock	500 mL
2	bay leaves	2
3	beets, peeled and cut into ½-inch (1 cm) cubes	3
2	potatoes, peeled and cut into ½-inch (1 cm) cubes	2
1½ cups	frozen green peas, thawed	375 mL
¼ cup	tomato chutney	50 mL
	Finely chopped cilantro	
	Finely chopped long green chilies (optional)	

1. In a dry skillet, over medium heat, toast cumin seeds until they release their aroma and just begin to turn brown. Transfer to a mortar or a spice grinder and grind coarsely. Set aside.

2. In the same skillet, heat oil over medium heat. Add onions and cook, stirring, until softened. Add garlic, salt, peppercorns and reserved cumin and cook, stirring for 1 minute. Add vegetable stock and bay leaves and bring to a boil. Place beets and potatoes in stoneware and add onion mixture.

3. Cover and cook on **Low** for 8 hours or on **High** for 4 hours, until vegetables are tender. Add peas, stir to blend and cook on **High** for 15 minutes, until peas are tender. Stir in chutney. Ladle into bowls and garnish with cilantro and chilies, if using.

Parsnip and Coconut Curry with Crispy Shallots

SERVES 6

• • • • •

The combination of sweet parsnips, spicy curry, mellow coconut milk and crispy shallots is absolutely delicious. I like to serve this over hot rice or with a warm Indian bread such as naan, alongside a small platter of stir-fried bok choy, drizzled with toasted sesame oil and sprinkled with toasted sesame seeds.

• • • • •

Make ahead

This dish can be partially prepared the night before it is cooked. Complete Step 1. Cover and refrigerate overnight. The next morning, continue cooking as directed in Step 2.

1 tbsp	vegetable oil	15 mL
1	large onion, fined chopped	1
4	stalks celery, thinly sliced	4
6	parsnips, peeled and diced	6
1 tbsp	minced gingerroot	15 mL
2 tsp	curry powder	10 mL
2 tsp	cumin seeds	10 mL
1 cup	vegetable stock	250 mL
1 cup	coconut milk	250 mL
1 cup	green peas, thawed if frozen	250 mL

CRISPY SHALLOT TOPPING

2 tbsp	vegetable oil	25 mL
½ cup	diced shallots	125 mL

1. In a skillet, heat oil over medium heat. Add onion, celery and parsnips and cook, stirring, until softened, about 7 minutes. Add gingerroot, curry powder and cumin seeds and cook, stirring for 1 minute. Stir in vegetable stock.

2. Transfer mixture to slow cooker stoneware. Cover and cook on **Low** for 8 hours or **High** for 4 hours, until vegetables are tender. Stir in coconut milk and green peas. Cover and cook on **High** for 20 to 30 minutes until peas are cooked and mixture is bubbling.

3. Crispy Shallot Topping: In a skillet, heat oil over medium-high heat. Add shallots and cook, stirring until they are browned and crispy, about 5 minutes. Ladle curry into individual serving bowls and top with shallots.

Vegetable Goulash

SERVES 4

• • • • •

This hearty and delicious stew is the perfect pick-me-up after a day in the chilly outdoors. Serve over hot cooked noodles. topped with a dollop of sour cream, if desired. Accompany with dark rye bread and a salad of shredded carrots. For a special occasion, top with puff pastry and transform it into Vegetable Pot Pie (see Variation, right).

• • • • •

Make ahead

This dish can be partially prepared the night before it is cooked. Complete Steps 1, 2 and 3. Cover and refrigerate overnight. The next morning, continue with Step 4.

4	dried shiitake mushrooms	4
2 tbsp	vegetable oil, divided	25 mL
8 oz	fresh shiitake mushrooms, stems removed and coarsely chopped	250 g
I	onion, finely chopped	I
4	stalks celery, diced	4
2	each carrots and parsnips, peeled and diced	2
2 tsp	paprika	10 mL
I tsp	caraway seeds, coarsely crushed	5 mL
½ tsp	each salt and cracked black peppercorns	2 mL
I tbsp	all-purpose flour	15 mL
2 cups	vegetable stock	500 mL
I	green bell pepper, seeded and diced	I

1. Soak mushrooms in 1 cup (250 mL) boiling water for 30 minutes. Drain and pat dry. Cut into quarters.

2. In a skillet, heat 1 tbsp (15 mL) oil over medium heat. Add fresh mushrooms and cook, stirring, just until they begin to soften. Transfer to slow cooker stoneware.

3. Heat remaining oil in pan. Add onion, celery, carrots and parsnips and cook, stirring, until softened, about 5 minutes. Add paprika, caraway seeds, salt, peppercorns and dried shiitake mushrooms and cook, stirring, for 1 minute. Add flour and cook, stirring, for 1 minute. Add stock and cook, stirring, until thickened, 3 minutes. Transfer to slow cooker stoneware.

4. Cover and cook on **Low** for 6 hours or on **High** for 3 hours, until vegetables are tender. Add pepper. Cover and cook on **High** until soft, about 15 minutes.

Variation

Vegetable Pot Pie

If desired, add ½ cup (125 mL) whipping (35%) cream to the cooked goulash. Ladle into a casserole dish or 4 ovenproof ramekins. Top with thawed prepared puff pastry, cut to fit. Bake for 20 to 25 minutes in a 400°F (200°C) oven, until pastry is puffed and browned.

Sweet Potato Curry with Mushrooms and Eggplant

SERVES 6 TO 8

• • • • •

This unusual combination is both delicious and nutritious. Serve over rice and accompany with steamed spinach sprinkled with sesame seeds for a finishing touch.

• • • • •

Tip

I have not included a quantity of salt in the recipe because there is likely residual salt in the sweated eggplant. Be sure to taste the mixture once the vegetables have been combined and add salt cautiously, to taste.

• • • • •

Make ahead

This dish can be partially prepared the night before it is cooked. Complete Steps 1, 2 and 3. Cover and refrigerate overnight. The next morning, continue with Step 4.

1	medium eggplant, peeled, cut into 1-inch (2.5 cm) cubes and sweated and drained of excess moisture (see Tips, page 23)	1
2 tsp	coriander seeds	10 mL
2 tsp	cumin seeds	10 mL
1 tbsp	vegetable oil (approx.)	15 mL
2	medium sweet potatoes, cut into ½-inch (1 cm) cubes	2
2	medium portobello mushrooms, stems removed, cut into quarters and ¼-inch (0.5 cm) slices	2
2	onions, finely chopped	2
4	cloves garlic, finely chopped	4
1 tsp	cracked black peppercorns	5 mL
1	can (19 oz/540 mL) tomatoes, including juice, coarsely chopped	1
	Salt, to taste	
1	long red or green chili or Thai chili, finely chopped (optional)	1
½ cup	plain yogurt (optional)	125 mL

1. In a dry skillet, toast coriander and cumin seeds until they release their aroma and start to brown. Transfer to a spice grinder or mortar, or use the bottom of a measuring cup or wine bottle to coarsely grind. Set aside.

2. In a nonstick skillet, heat oil over medium heat. Add sweated eggplant and cook until lightly browned. Transfer to slow cooker stoneware. Add sweet potatoes and mushrooms and stir to combine.

3. Add onions to pan, adding additional oil if necessary, and cook, stirring, until softened, about 3 minutes. Add garlic, reserved coriander and cumin and peppercorns and cook, stirring, for 1 minute. Stir in tomatoes with juice and bring to a boil. Pour over eggplant mixture and stir to combine. Add salt.

4. Cover and cook on **Low** for 8 hours or on **High** for 4 hours, until hot and bubbling. Stir in chili pepper and yogurt, if using, and serve immediately.

Braised Fennel with Parsnips

SERVES 4

• • • • •

Although unusual, this combination of fennel and parsnips, with a hint of caraway, is very tasty. I like to serve this over fluffy garlic mashed potatoes, topped with shaved Parmesan and accompanied by a simple green salad.

• • • • •

Tip

Crush caraway or fennel seeds in a mortar with a pestle or on a cutting board using the bottom of a measuring cup.

• • • • •

Make ahead

This dish can be partially prepared the night before it is served. Complete Step 1. Cover and refrigerate overnight. The next morning, continue cooking as directed in Step 2.

1 tbsp	vegetable oil	15 mL
2	onions, finely chopped	2
6	parsnips, peeled and cut into ¼-inch (0.5 cm) slices	6
2	fennel bulbs, base and leafy stems discarded, bulb thinly sliced on the vertical	2
3	cloves garlic, minced	3
1 tsp	caraway seeds, coarsely crushed (see Tip, left)	5 mL
1 tsp	salt	5 mL
½ tsp	cracked black peppercorns	2 mL
1 tbsp	all-purpose flour	15 mL
1¼ cups	tomato juice	300 mL
1 cup	frozen green peas, thawed	250 mL

1. In a skillet, heat oil over medium heat. Add onions, parsnips and fennel and cook, stirring, until vegetables are softened, about 7 minutes. Add garlic, caraway seeds, salt and peppercorns and cook, stirring, for 1 minute. Add flour and cook, stirring, for 1 minute. Add tomato juice and cook, stirring, until mixture begins to thicken, about 2 minutes.

2. Cover and cook on **Low** for 6 to 8 hours or on **High** for 3 to 4 hours, until mixture is hot and bubbling. Stir in peas. Cover and cook on **High** until peas are tender, about 15 minutes.

Creamy Braised Fennel

SERVES 4

* * * * *

The sauce is the highlight of this dish, rich and complex with the intriguing, slightly bitter taste of saffron. Serve this over mashed potatoes, rice, polenta or grits or, for something completely different, a white bean purée (see Tip, below).

* * * * *

Tip

Easy White Bean Purée: Heat 1 tbsp (15 mL) oil in a skillet over medium heat. Add ½ cup (125 mL) chopped parsley and 2 cloves of minced garlic and cook, stirring, for 1 minute. Add 1 can (14 to 19 oz/398 to 540 mL) white kidney beans, drained and rinsed and cook, mashing with a fork, until beans are heated through. Season to taste with salt and freshly ground black pepper.

* * * * *

Make ahead

This dish can be assembled the night before it is cooked. Complete Steps 1 and 2. Cover and refrigerate overnight. The next morning, continue cooking as directed in Step 3.

⅛ tsp	saffron threads	0.5 mL
1 tbsp	vegetable oil	15 mL
1	medium onion, finely chopped	1
2	medium carrots, peeled and diced	2
2	stalks celery, diced	2
2	cloves garlic, finely chopped	2
1 tsp	salt	5 mL
½ tsp	whole fennel seeds, coarsely crushed (see Tip, page 92)	2 mL
½ tsp	crushed black peppercorns	2 mL
1 cup	vegetable stock	250 mL
4	fennel bulbs, base and leafy stems discarded, bulb thinly sliced on the vertical	4
½ cup	dry white wine or vermouth	125 mL
2 tbsp	freshly squeezed lemon juice	25 mL
2 tbsp	whipping (35 %) cream	25 mL
2 tbsp	freshly grated Parmesan cheese	25 mL

1. Crumble saffron between your thumb and fingers into a small bowl. Add 1 tbsp (15 mL) boiling water and stir well. Set aside.

2. In a skillet, heat oil over medium heat. Add onion, carrots and celery and cook, stirring, until softened, about 7 minutes. Add garlic, salt, fennel seeds and peppercorns and cook, stirring, for 1 minute. Stir in saffron water and vegetable stock. Place fennel in slow cooker. Add vegetable mixture.

3. Cover and cook for 7 to 8 hours on **Low** or 3 to 4 hours on **High**, until fennel is tender.

4. Using a slotted spoon, transfer fennel to a heatproof serving dish and keep warm in oven. Pour liquid from slow cooker into a large saucepan. Add white wine, lemon juice and cream and bring to a boil over medium-high heat. Continue cooking until liquid is reduced by a third, about 6 minutes. Add Parmesan and stir until melted. Taste and adjust seasoning. Pour over fennel and serve.

Tofu Ratatouille

SERVE 6 TO 8

• • • • •

Like any good ratatouille, this one involves quite a bit of preparation. Although it is time-consuming, sautéeing the vegetables individually ensures that their individual flavors aren't lost when the dish is complete. The results are worth the extra effort. Serve this to your most discriminating guests and expect requests for seconds.

• • • • •

Tips

I have not included a quantity of salt in this recipe because there is likely to be some residual salt left on the eggplant and zucchini after sweating. I recommend that you taste and under-salt the tomato mixture before adding it to the slow cooker. If there isn't enough, you can always add salt once the cooking is completed.

RATATOUILLE

1	large eggplant, peeled, cut into 1/4-inch (0.5 cm) cubes, and sweated and drained of excess moisture (see Tips, page 23)	1
2 tbsp	vegetable oil, divided	25 mL
8 oz	mushrooms, stems removed and quartered	250 g
2	small zucchini, thinly sliced, sweated and rinsed	2
1	large onion, finely chopped	1
3	cloves garlic, minced	3
1/2 tsp	cracked black peppercorns	2 mL
1/2 tsp	dried thyme leaves	2 mL
1/2 tsp	ground cinnamon	2 mL
1	can (28 oz/796 mL) tomatoes, including juice, coarsely chopped	1
	Salt, to taste	

TOFU

8 oz	firm tofu with fine herbs, cut into 1-inch (2.5 cm) cubes	250 g
	Salt and freshly ground black pepper, to taste	
1 tbsp	vegetable oil	15 mL

1. Ratatouille: In a skillet, heat 1 tbsp (15 mL) oil over medium heat. Add mushrooms and cook, stirring, just until they begin to lose their liquid. Using a slotted spoon, transfer to slow cooker stoneware. Return pan to element and add more oil, if needed.

2. Add zucchini in batches and cook, stirring, until it softens and begins to brown. Using a slotted spoon, transfer to a bowl. Cover and refrigerate.

If you are too busy to cook at the end of the day, fry the tofu when you cook the zucchini. Cover and refrigerate. Add to the slow cooker along with the zucchini and cook until heated through.

• • • • •

Make ahead

This dish can be partially prepared the night before it is cooked. Complete Steps 1 through 3. Cover and refrigerate overnight. The next morning continue cooking as directed in Step 4.

3. Add eggplant to pan, in batches, and sauté, until lightly browned, adding more oil as needed. Transfer to slow cooker as completed. Add onion to pan and cook, stirring, until softened. Add garlic, peppercorns, thyme and cinnamon and cook, stirring for 1 minute. Add tomatoes with juice and bring to a boil. Pour over contents of slow cooker. Stir to blend.

4. Cover and cook on **Low** for 8 hours or **High** for 4 hours, until hot and bubbling. Add reserved zucchini and cook on **High**, until heated through, about 15 minutes.

5. Tofu: Season tofu with salt and pepper. In a skillet, heat oil over medium heat. Add tofu and cook, stirring, until lightly browned, about 15 minutes. Spread tofu over top of eggplant mixture and serve immediately.

Braised Leeks with Celery Root

SERVES 4

• • • • •

Leeks and celery root make a great combination. I like to serve this over Champ, Irish-style mashed potatoes made with scallion-infused milk, but a cooked grain, such as polenta, would also work well. This dish is tasty on its own or with just a sprinkling of Parmesan, but if you're feeling the need for an enhancement add the Horseradish Cream.

• • • • •

Make ahead

This dish can be assembled the night before it is cooked. Complete Steps 1 and 2. Cover and refrigerate overnight. The next morning, continue cooking as directed.

I	large celery root, peeled and julienned	I
2 tbsp	freshly squeezed lemon juice	25 mL
2 tbsp	butter or vegetable oil	25 mL
3	leeks, white part with a bit of green, cleaned and thinly sliced	3
I tbsp	minced garlic	15 mL
I tsp	salt	5 mL
½ tsp	freshly ground black pepper	2 mL
I	can (14 oz/398 mL) tomatoes, including juice	I
I tbsp	tomato paste	15 mL
	Freshly grated Parmesan cheese (optional)	

HORSERADISH CREAM (OPTIONAL)

½ cup	whipping (35%) cream	125 mL
2 tbsp	prepared horseradish	25 mL

1. In a bowl, toss celery root with lemon juice. Set aside.

2. In a skillet, melt butter or heat vegetable oil over medium-low heat. Add leeks and cook, stirring, until softened, about 4 minutes. Add garlic, salt and pepper and cook, stirring, for 1 minute. Add tomatoes with juice and tomato paste and bring to a boil. Transfer to slow cooker stoneware. Add reserved celery root and stir to combine.

3. Cover and cook on **Low** for 8 hours or on **High** for 4 hours. Serve immediately. Sprinkle with Parmesan cheese or top each serving with a dollop of Horseradish Cream, if using.

4. Horseradish Cream: In a bowl, whip cream. Fold in horseradish. Spoon into a bowl and pass at the table.

Mushroom and Artichoke Lasagna *page 72* ➤
Overleaf: Cheesy White Chili with Cauliflower *page 108*

Cheese and Corn Loaf

SERVES 6 TO 8

• • • • •

There is something quintessentially comforting about the combination of cheese and corn. Serve this tasty loaf with a tossed green or sliced tomato salad for a delightfully different meal.

• • • • •

Tips

If you don't have a loaf pan that fits into your slow cooker, try making this loaf in a round (6 cup/1.5 L) soufflé dish or a square (7 inch/17.5 cm) baking dish. Also, most supermarkets have a wide range of foil baking pans that fit easily into oval-shaped stoneware. Choose one that comes closest to the dimensions specified above.

If you prefer a spicier version of this loaf, add 1 finely chopped jalapeño pepper along with the green bell pepper.

• 8-by 5-inch (20 by 12.5 cm) loaf pan, lightly greased (see Tips, left)

8 oz	ricotta cheese	250 g
½ cup	freshly grated Parmesan cheese	125 mL
4	eggs, beaten	4
2 cups	corn kernels, thawed if frozen	500 mL
2 tbsp	butter	25 mL
3	leeks, white part only with a bit of green, cleaned and thinly sliced (see page 23)	3
3	cloves garlic, minced	3
¼ cup	diced green bell pepper	50 mL
1 tsp	salt	5 mL
½ tsp	dried thyme leaves	2 mL
	Freshly ground black pepper, to taste	
1 tbsp	all-purpose flour	15 mL
1 cup	vegetable stock	250 mL

1. In a bowl, combine ricotta, Parmesan and eggs. Beat with a wooden spoon until smooth. Fold in corn. Set aside.

2. In a skillet, melt butter over medium heat. Add leeks and cook, stirring, until softened, about 4 minutes. Add garlic, green pepper, salt, thyme and black pepper, and cook, stirring for 1 minute. Add flour and cook, stirring, for 1 minute. Add vegetable stock and cook, stirring, until thickened. Fold into cheese mixture. Spoon mixture into prepared loaf pan.

3. Cover with foil and secure with a string or elastic band. Place pan in slow cooker stoneware and pour in enough boiling water to reach 1 inch (2.5 cm) up the sides of the dish. Cover and cook on **High** for 4 hours until set. Serve warm.

◄ Cider Baked Beans *page 118*
Overleaf: Moors and Christians *page 112*

Potato Peanut Loaf

SERVES 4 TO 6

* * * * *

This unusual combination of potatoes and peanuts in a tasty loaf is a great antidote for tired taste buds. Add a tossed green salad to complete the meal.

* * * * *

Tips

Be sure the potatoes are cut in a small dice. Otherwise, the loaf may not hold together.

If you don't have tomato sauce, this loaf is also very tasty served with homemade chili sauce or another tomato-based relish, such as piccalilli.

* * * * *

Make ahead

This dish can be assembled the night before it is cooked. Complete Step 1. Refrigerate overnight. The next day, continue with Step 2.

• 8-by 5-inch (20 by 12.5 cm) loaf pan, lightly greased (see Tips, page 97)

6 cups	cooked, peeled and diced potatoes	1.5 L
1 cup	finely chopped roasted unsalted peanuts	250 mL
¼ cup	finely chopped green onion	50 mL
¼ cup	finely chopped parsley	50 mL
2	reconstituted sun-dried tomatoes, finely chopped	2
½ tsp	salt	2 mL
½ tsp	chili powder	2 mL
	Freshly ground black pepper, to taste	
2	eggs, beaten	2
½ cup	tomato-based chili sauce	125 mL
4 oz	cream cheese, diced and softened	125 g
¼ cup plus 2 tbsp	freshly grated Parmesan cheese, divided	75 mL
	Warm tomato sauce (optional) (see Tips, left)	

1. In a large bowl, combine potatoes, peanuts, green onions, parsley, sun-dried tomatoes, salt, chili powder and pepper. Mix well. Add eggs, chili sauce, cream cheese and ¼ cup (50 mL) Parmesan and mix well. Spoon into prepared pan and sprinkle remaining 2 tbsp (25 mL) Parmesan over top. Cover tightly with foil and secure with string or elastic band.

2. Place pan in slow cooker stoneware and pour in enough boiling water to come 1 inch (2.5 cm) up the sides. Cover and cook on **Low** for 8 hours or on **High** for 4 hours. Serve hot, topped with a dollop of tomato sauce, if using.

Beans and Lentils

Basic Beans

MAKES APPROXIMATELY 2 CUPS (500 ML) COOKED BEANS (SEE TIP, BELOW)

• • • • •

Loaded with nutrition and high in fiber, dried beans are one of our most healthful edibles. As a key ingredient in many of our best-loved dishes, they can also be absolutely delicious. The slow cooker excels at turning these unappetizing bullets into potentially sublime fare. It is also extraordinarily convenient — since discovering the slow cooker, I don't cook dried beans any other way. I put presoaked beans into the slow cooker before I go to bed and when I wake up, they are ready for whatever recipe I plan to make.

• • • • •

Tip

This recipe may be doubled or tripled to suit the quantity of beans required for a recipe.

| 1 cup | dried beans or chickpeas | 250 mL |
| 3 cups | water | 750 mL |

1. Long soak: In a bowl, combine beans and water. Soak for at least 6 hours or overnight. Drain and rinse thoroughly with cold water. Beans are now ready for cooking.

2. Quick soak: In a pot, combine beans and water. Cover and bring to a boil. Boil for 3 minutes. Turn off heat and soak for 1 hour. Drain and rinse thoroughly under cold water. Beans are now ready to cook.

3. Cooking: In slow cooker, combine 1 cup (250 mL) presoaked beans and 3 cups (750 mL) fresh cold water. Season with garlic, bay leaves or a bouquet garni made from your favorite herbs tied together in a cheesecloth, if desired. Add salt to taste. Cover and cook on **Low** for 10 to 12 hours or overnight. Drain and rinse. If not using immediately, cover and refrigerate. The beans are now ready for use in your favorite recipe.

Legumes (Dried beans and lentils)
Once cooked, legumes should be covered and stored in the refrigerator, where they will keep for four to five days. Cooked legumes can also be frozen in an airtight container. They will keep frozen for up to six months.

Storing Legumes
Dried beans and lentils should be stored in a dry, airtight container at room temperature. Since they lose their moisture over time, they are best used within a year. You'll know your beans are stale if their skins shrivel up when they are soaked.

Substitutions
Canned beans are a quick and easy substitute for cooked dried beans. Although the sizes of canned beans vary, the differences won't effect the results of most recipes. For 2 cups (500 mL) cooked beans, use a standard can, which usually range in size from 14 oz (398 mL) to 19 oz (540 mL). Rinse well under cold running water before adding to your recipe.

Red Beans and Rice

SERVES 6

• • • • •

This is a North American version of that classic combination of beans and rice, which turns up in many cuisines. Accompanied by a salad or green vegetable, it makes a great main course. It can also do double duty as a side dish.

• • • • •

Tips

For a more robustly flavored result, use Enhanced Vegetable Stock (see recipe, page 38) in this recipe.

If you prefer a bit a smoke with your spice, substitute a chipotle chili (or two!) in adobo sauce for the jalapeño.

• • • • •

Make ahead

This dish can be partially prepared the night before it is cooked. Complete Steps 1 and 2. Cover and refrigerate overnight. The next morning, continue with Step 3.

1 cup	dry red beans, such as kidney, pinto, cranberry or romano	250 mL
1 tbsp	vegetable oil	15 mL
2	onions, finely chopped	2
4	stalks celery, peeled and diced	4
6	cloves garlic, minced	6
1 tsp	dried oregano leaves	5 mL
1 tsp	salt	5 mL
½ tsp	cracked black peppercorns	2 mL
3 cups	vegetable stock (see Tips, left)	750 mL
1 to 2	jalapeño peppers, finely chopped	1 to 2
1	green bell pepper, chopped	1
1 tbsp	red wine vinegar (optional)	15 mL
1 cup	long-grain white rice, cooked	250 mL
	Finely chopped green onion, parsley or cilantro	
	Hot pepper sauce (optional)	

1. Soak beans according to either method in Basic Beans (see page 100). Drain and rinse and set aside.

2. In a skillet, heat oil over medium heat. Add onions and celery and cook, stirring, until softened, about 5 minutes. Add garlic, oregano, salt and peppercorns and cook, stirring, for 1 minute. Add beans and stir to coat. Transfer to slow cooker stoneware. Add vegetable stock and stir well.

3. Cover and cook on **Low** for 8 to 10 hours, until beans are tender. Add jalapeño peppers, green pepper and vinegar, if using. Cover and cook on **High** for 20 minutes, until pepper is tender. Stir in rice, garnish with green onion and serve with hot pepper sauce, if desired.

A winner on "on 4 HR" setting took 3 HRS

Brown Rice and Beans with Cheese and Chilies

SERVES 6

• • • • •

Not only does this delicious casserole appeal to a wide variety of tastes, the combination of rice and beans creates a complete protein, making it particularly nutritious. Add a tossed salad and hot crusty rolls for a satisfying meal.

• • • • •

Tips

Substitute cranberry, Romano, pinto or red kidney beans for the black beans, if desired.

For a more robust flavor, use Enhanced Vegetable Stock (see recipe, page 38) in this recipe.

Accumulated moisture affects the consistency of the rice. The tea towels will absorb the moisture generated during cooking.

• • • • •

Make ahead

This dish can be assembled the night before it is cooked. Complete Step 1. Cover and refrigerate overnight. The next morning, continue cooking as directed.

1 tbsp	vegetable oil	15 mL
1	onion, finely chopped	1
2	stalks celery, peeled and diced	2
¾ cup	long-grain brown rice	175 mL
½ tsp	salt	2 mL
½ tsp	cracked black peppercorns	2 mL
1	can (10 oz/284 mL) condensed, cream of celery soup	1
1½ cups	vegetable stock	375 mL
1	can (14 to 19 oz/398 to 540 mL) black beans, drained and rinsed, or 1 cup (250 mL) dried black beans, cooked and drained (see Basic Beans, page 100)	1
1	jalapeño pepper, finely chopped (optional)	1
1	can (4.5 oz/127 mL) mild green chilies, chopped	1
2½ cups	shredded Cheddar cheese	625 mL

1. In a skillet, heat oil over medium heat. Add onion and celery and cook, stirring, until softened, about 5 minutes. Add rice, salt and peppercorns and cook, stirring, for 1 minute. Add soup and stock and stir until smooth. Stir in beans and transfer to slow cooker stoneware.

2. Place two clean tea towels, each folded in half (so you will have four layers), over top of stoneware, to absorb the accumulated moisture. Cover and cook on **Low** for 8 hours or on **High** for 4 hours, until hot and bubbling.

3. Remove tea towels. Add jalapeño pepper, if using, green chilies and Cheddar cheese. Cover and cook on **High** for 20 to 30 minutes, until cheese is melted and mixture is hot and bubbling.

Moussaka with Tofu Topping

SERVES 6

• • • • •

This delicious rendition of the classic Greek dish, with an unusual tofu topping, is every bit as good as the original.

• • • • •

Tips

If you are using a canned or bottled tomato sauce that is a little more or less than the quantity suggested, don't worry. Excellent results have been produced using as little as 2¾ cups (675 mL) to as much as 3¼ cups (800 mL) tomato sauce.

Tofu comes in various textures. Soft or silken tofu works best in sauces, spreads and shakes. Firmer tofu hold its texture in dishes such as stir-fries. Tofu in the mid-range of firmness works best in this topping.

• • • • •

Make ahead

This dish can be partially assembled the night before it is cooked. Complete Steps 1 through 3. Cover and refrigerate overnight. The next morning, continue with Step 4.

2	eggplants, peeled, cut into 2-inch (5 cm) cubes, and sweated and drained of excess moisture (see Tips, page 23)	2
¼ cup	vegetable oil	50 mL
2	onions, finely chopped	2
4	cloves garlic, minced	4
1 tsp	dried oregano leaves	5 mL
1 tsp	cumin seeds	5 mL
½ tsp	salt	2 mL
½ tsp	cracked black peppercorns	2 mL
1	can (14 to 19 oz/398 to 540 mL) chickpeas, drained and rinsed, or 1 cup (250 mL) dried chickpeas, cooked and drained (see Basic Beans, page 100)	1
3 cups	tomato sauce	750 mL

TOPPING

1 lb	medium tofu	500 g
2	eggs	2
½ cup	freshly grated Parmesan cheese	125 mL
Pinch	each ground nutmeg and cinnamon	Pinch

1. In a skillet, heat oil over medium heat. Add eggplant, in batches, and cook until browned. Set aside.

2. Add onions to pan and cook, stirring, until softened, about 3 minutes. Add garlic, oregano, cumin seeds, salt and peppercorns and cook, stirring, for 1 minute. Add chickpeas and stir well.

3. Spread 1 cup (250 mL) tomato sauce evenly over bottom of slow cooker stoneware. Spread one-third of the eggplant over sauce and half of the chickpea mixture over eggplant. Repeat. Finish with remaining eggplant and pour remaining tomato sauce over top.

4. Topping: In a food processor or blender, purée tofu, eggs, Parmesan, nutmeg and cinnamon. Spread over eggplant. To prevent moisture from dripping on the topping, place tea towels over top of slow cooker stoneware. Cover and cook on **Low** for 6 to 8 hours or on **High** for 3 to 4 hours.

Two-Bean Chili with Zucchini

SERVES 6

• • • • •

Loaded with healthy vegetables and beans, vegetarian chili is a great dish for those of us who are trying to eat less fat and increase dietary fiber. This delicious version combines fresh green beans with dried beans and adds corn kernels and sautéed zucchini for a tasty finish.

• • • • •

Tips

Substitute cranberry, Romano or red kidney beans for the pinto beans, if desired.

Crush cumin seeds in a mortar with a pestle or on a cutting board, using the bottom of a measuring cup.

• • • • •

Make ahead

This chili can be partially prepared the night before it is cooked. Complete Steps 1 through 3. Cover and refrigerate overnight. The next morning, continue with Step 4.

2	small zucchini, cut into $1/2$-inch (1 cm) lengths and sweated	2
2	dried ancho chili peppers	2
2 cups	boiling water	500 mL
1 tbsp	vegetable oil	15 mL
2	onions, finely chopped	2
2	cloves garlic, minced	2
1 tbsp	cumin seeds, coarsely chopped (see Tips, left)	15 mL
1 tbsp	dried oregano leaves	15 mL
1 tsp	salt	5 mL
$1/2$ tsp	cracked black peppercorns	2 mL
1	can (28 oz/796 mL) tomatoes, including juice, coarsely chopped	1
2 cups	green beans, cut into 2-inch (5 cm) lengths	500 mL
1	can (14 to 19 oz/398 to 540 mL) pinto beans, drained and rinsed, or 1 cup (250 mL) dried pinto beans, cooked and drained (see Basic Beans, page 100)	1
$1 1/2$ cups	corn kernels	375 mL
1 cup	shredded Monterey Jack cheese (optional)	250 mL
	Sour cream (optional)	
	Finely chopped cilantro	

1. In a heatproof bowl, soak ancho chilies in boiling water for 30 minutes. Drain, discarding soaking liquid and stems. Pat dry, chop finely and set aside.

2. In a skillet, heat oil over medium heat. Add zucchini and cook, stirring, until it begins to brown. Transfer to a bowl using a slotted spoon, cover and refrigerate.

3. In same skillet, add onions and cook, stirring, until softened, about 3 minutes. Add garlic, cumin seeds, oregano, reserved ancho chilies, salt and peppercorns and cook, stirring, for 1 minute. Add tomatoes with juice and green beans and bring to a boil. Transfer to slow cooker stoneware. Add beans and stir to combine.

4. Cover and cook on **Low** for 8 hours or on **High** for 4 hours, until mixture is bubbling and hot. Stir in corn and reserved zucchini. Cover and cook on **High** for 20 minutes, until zucchini is heated through. Ladle into bowls and top with cheese or sour cream, if using. Garnish with cilantro.

Three-Bean Chili with Bulgur

SERVES 10 TO 12

• • • • • •

Here is a big-batch vegetarian chili so rich and thick your guests won't know it doesn't contain meat unless you tell them. The secret is the portobello mushrooms, which add hearty flavor, and the bulgur, which thickens the sauce and adds texture to the chili. Garnish with any combination of chopped avocado, sliced red onion, shredded Monterey Jack cheese and finely chopped cilantro for a tasty and healthy meal.

• • • • • •

Tips

Like all chilies, this recipe reheats well. However, you can halve this recipe if the quantity is too large for you.

If, like me, you particularly enjoy the taste of cumin, toast the cumin seeds and lightly crush them before adding to the mixture. In a large dry skillet, toast cumin seeds until they release their aroma. Transfer to a spice grinder or mortar, or use the bottom of a measuring cup or wine bottle to coarsely grind.

1 tbsp	vegetable oil	15 mL
2	onions, finely chopped	2
4	carrots, peeled and diced	4
4	stalks celery, peeled and diced	4
4	cloves garlic, minced	4
2 tbsp	chili powder	25 mL
1 tbsp	dried oregano leaves	15 mL
1 tbsp	cumin seeds, coarsely chopped (see Tips, left)	15 mL
2 tsp	salt	10 mL
1 tsp	cracked black peppercorns	5 mL
1	can (28 oz/796 mL) tomatoes, including juice	1
3	large portobello mushrooms, stemmed and cut into 1/2-inch (1 cm) squares	3
3 cups	vegetable stock	750 mL
1	can (14 to 19 oz/398 to 540 mL) white kidney beans, drained and rinsed, or 1 cup (250 mL) dried white kidney beans, cooked and drained (see Basic Beans, page 100)	1
1	can (14 to 19 oz/398 to 540 mL) red kidney beans, drained and rinsed, or 1 cup (250 mL) dried red kidney beans, cooked and drained	1
1	can (14 to 19 oz/398 to 540 mL) chickpeas, drained and rinsed, or 1 cup (250 mL) dried chickpeas, cooked and drained	1
1 to 2	jalapeño peppers, seeded and finely chopped	1 to 2
1 cup	bulgur	250 mL

This recipe showcases a variety of dried beans, which, in addition to being easily stored pantry ingredients, are one of our most healthful foods. Legumes, a category that includes lentils as well as dried beans, are a rich source of B vitamins, calcium, iron, phosphorous, potassium and zinc. They are also an excellent source of fiber and low-fat protein. Bulgur, a grain made from cracked wheat that has been roasted, completes the range of essential amino acids in the beans, making this a particularly nutritious dish for vegetarians as it is a complete protein.

* * * * *

Make ahead

This dish can be partially prepared the night before it is cooked. Complete Step 1. Cover and refrigerate overnight. The next morning, continue with Step 2.

1. In a skillet, heat oil over medium heat. Add onions, carrots and celery and cook, stirring, until softened, about 7 minutes. Add garlic, chili powder, oregano, cumin seeds, salt and peppercorns and cook, stirring, for 1 minute. Add tomatoes with juice, and bring to a boil, breaking up with a spoon. Place mushrooms in stoneware. Pour mixture over mushrooms. Add vegetable stock, white and red kidney beans and chickpeas and stir to combine.

2. Cover and cook on **Low** for 8 to 10 hours or on **High** for 4 to 5 hours, until mixture is hot and bubbling. Stir in jalapeño pepper and bulgur. Cover and cook until bulgur absorbs liquid and is tender, about 30 minutes. Serve hot.

Cheesy White Chili with Cauliflower

SERVES 6 TO 8

• • • • •

This pale vegetarian chili is both pretty to look at and delicious to eat. Add the cream cheese if you prefer a thicker, cheesier sauce, and the mild green chilies for a flavor boost. Serve with hot crusty bread and a salad of sliced tomatoes in vinaigrette for a great meal.

• • • • •

Tips

If you prefer a thicker chili, mash some or all of the beans or purée in a food processor before adding to the recipe.

If you are assembling this chili the night before you plan to serve it, for convenience, chop the peppers and cook the cauliflower, as well. Cover and refrigerate until ready to add to the recipe in Step 3.

• • • • •

Make ahead

This chili can be partially prepared the night before it is cooked. Complete Step 1. Cover and refrigerate overnight. The next morning, continue cooking as directed.

1 tbsp	vegetable oil	15 mL
2	onions, finely chopped	2
4	cloves garlic, minced	4
1 tbsp	cumin seeds	15 mL
1 tbsp	dried oregano leaves	15 mL
1 tbsp	chili powder	15 mL
1 tsp	salt	5 mL
½ tsp	cracked black peppercorns	2 mL
1	can (14 to 19 oz/398 to 540 mL) white kidney beans, drained and rinsed, or 1 cup (250 mL) dried white kidney beans, cooked and drained	1
3 cups	vegetable stock	750 mL
3 cups	cauliflower florets, cooked for 4 minutes in salted boiling water and drained	750 mL
1 to 2	jalapeño peppers, minced	1 to 2
1	green bell pepper, diced	1
2 cups	shredded Monterey Jack cheese	500 mL
4 oz	cream cheese, cut into ½-inch (1 cm) cubes and softened (optional)	125 g
1	can (4.5 oz/127 mL) chopped mild green chilies (optional)	1
	Finely chopped green onions (optional)	
	Finely chopped cilantro (optional)	

1. In a skillet, heat oil over medium heat. Add onions and cook, stirring, until softened, about 3 minutes. Add garlic, cumin seeds, oregano, chili powder, salt and peppercorns and cook, stirring, for 1 minute. Transfer mixture to slow cooker stoneware. Add beans and stock and stir to combine.

2. Cover and cook on **Low** for 8 to 10 hours or on **High** for 4 to 5 hours, until hot and bubbling.

3. Stir in cauliflower, jalapeño pepper, green pepper, Monterey Jack cheese, and cream cheese and chilies, if using. Cover and cook on **High** for 25 to 30 minutes, until green peppers are softened and cauliflower is heated through. Ladle into bowls and garnish as desired.

Tuscan-Style Beans with Rosemary

SERVES 6 TO 8

* * * * *

I love this simple combination of white kidney beans seasoned with vegetables and herbs. Serve with a tossed green salad or tomatoes in vinaigrette for a perfect evening meal, or as an accompaniment to a more substantial main dish.

* * * * *

Tips

Use Enhanced Vegetable Stock (see recipe, page 38) for the best flavor.

For a change, top with toasted bread crumbs (see Variation, page 136).

* * * * *

Make ahead

This dish can be assembled the night before it is cooked. Complete Step 1. Cover and refrigerate overnight. The next day, continue cooking as directed in Step 2. Alternately, beans may be cooked overnight in slow cooker, refrigerated the following morning and reheated later on the stovetop. In a Dutch oven, bring to a boil and simmer for 5 to 10 minutes before serving.

I tbsp	olive oil	15 mL
I	large red onion, finely chopped	I
4	cloves garlic, minced	4
I	large potato, peeled and grated	I
2	sprigs fresh rosemary or I tbsp (15 mL) dried rosemary leaves	2
½ tsp	salt	2 mL
½ tsp	cracked black peppercorns	2 mL
I	can (28 oz/796 mL) tomatoes, including juice, coarsely chopped (see Tip, page 46)	I
2	cans (each 14 to 19 oz/398 to 540 mL) white kidney beans, drained and rinsed, or 2 cups (500 mL) dried white kidney beans, cooked and drained (see Basic Beans, page 100)	2
	Vegetable stock (see Tips, left)	
¼ cup	whole parsley leaves	50 mL

1. In a skillet, heat oil over medium heat. Add onion to pan and cook, stirring, just until it begins to soften, about 3 minutes. Add garlic, potato, rosemary, salt and peppercorns. Cook, stirring, for 1 minute. Stir in tomatoes with juice and bring to a boil. Cook, stirring until liquid is reduced by approximately one-third, about 2 minutes. Add beans to slow cooker stoneware. Pour contents of pan over beans and stir well. Add vegetable stock, barely to cover.

2. Cover and cook on **Low** for 8 to 10 hours or on **High** for 4 to 5 hours, until hot and bubbling. Stir in parsley and serve.

Light Chili

SERVES 4 TO 6

• • • • •

This is my favorite light chili. I love the rich, creamy sauce and the flavors of the spices. Serve this with a good dollop of sour cream, your favorite salsa and a sprinkling of chopped cilantro.

• • • • •

Make ahead

This dish can be partially prepared the night before it is served. Chop jalapeño and bell peppers and shred cheese. Cover and refrigerate. Complete Steps 1 and 2, cover and refrigerate overnight. The next morning, continue cooking as directed in Step 3.

1 tbsp	cumin seeds	15 mL
1 tbsp	vegetable oil	15 mL
2	onions, finely chopped	2
6	cloves garlic, minced	6
1 tbsp	dried oregano leaves	15 mL
1 tsp	each salt and cracked black peppercorns	5 mL
1	can (28 oz/796 mL) tomatoes, including juice, chopped (see Tip, page 46)	1
2 cups	vegetable stock	500 mL
8 oz	portobello mushrooms, stems removed, cut into 1-inch (2.5 cm) cubes	250 g
1	can (14 to 19 oz/398 to 540 mL) white kidney beans, rinsed and drained, or 1 cup (250 mL) dried white kidney beans, soaked, cooked and drained (see Basic Beans, page 100)	1
1 to 2	jalapeño peppers, finely chopped	1 to 2
2	green bell peppers, diced	2
1½ cups	shredded Monterey Jack cheese	375 mL
1	can (4½ oz/127 mL) diced mild green chilies, drained	1
	Sour cream	
	Salsa	
	Finely chopped cilantro	

1. In a large dry skillet, toast cumin seeds until they release their aroma. Transfer to a spice grinder or mortar, or use the bottom of a measuring cup or wine bottle to coarsely grind. Set aside.

2. In same skillet, heat oil over medium heat. Add onions and cook, stirring, until softened, about 3 minutes. Add garlic, oregano, salt, peppercorns and reserved cumin and cook, stirring, for 1 minute. Add tomatoes with juice and stock and bring to a boil. Cook, stirring, until liquid is reduced by one-third, about 5 minutes. Add mushrooms and beans to stoneware and pour tomato mixture over them. Stir to combine.

3. Cover and cook on **Low** for 6 to 8 hours or on **High** for 3 to 4 hours, until mixture is hot and bubbling. Stir in jalapeño peppers, green pepper, cheese and mild green chilies. Cover and cook on **High** for 20 to 30 minutes, until pepper is tender and cheese is melted. Ladle into bowls and top with sour cream, salsa and chopped cilantro.

Moors and Christians

SERVES 8

• • • • •

Although I've come across several different versions of how this classic Cuban dish got its name, all lead back to the eighth century when Spain was invaded by their enemies, the Moors. For a genuine Cuban touch, spoon onto plates, top with a fried egg and accompany with Fried Plantains (see Tips, right). I guarantee you'll have requests for seconds. This dish is also delicious cold and makes a nice addition to a buffet as a rice salad.

• • • • •

Tips

To roast peppers: Preheat oven to 400°F (200°C). Place pepper(s) on a baking sheet and roast, turning two or three times, until the skin on all sides is blackened. (This will take about 25 minutes.) Transfer pepper(s) to a heatproof bowl. Cover with a plate and let stand until cool. Remove and, using a sharp knife, lift skins off. Discard skins and slice according to recipe instructions.

1	roasted red bell pepper, finely chopped (see Tips, left)	1
1 tbsp	vegetable oil	15 mL
2	onions, finely chopped	2
4	large cloves garlic, minced	4
2 tsp	dried oregano leaves	10 mL
2 tsp	cumin seeds, coarsely crushed (see Tips, right)	10 mL
1	tomato, peeled, seeded and chopped	1
1	can (14 to 19 oz/398 to 540 mL) black beans, rinsed and drained, or 1 cup (250 mL) dried black beans, cooked and drained (see Basic Beans, page 100)	1
½ cup	vegetable stock	125 mL
2 cups	long-grain rice	500 mL
1	green bell pepper, finely chopped	1
2 tbsp	freshly squeezed lemon or lime juice	25 mL
¼ cup	finely chopped cilantro	50 mL
4	green onions, white part only, finely chopped	4

1. In a skillet, heat oil over medium heat. Add onion and cook, stirring, until softened, about 3 minutes. Add garlic, oregano and cumin seeds and cook, stirring, for 1 minute. Stir in tomato, beans and stock and bring to a boil. Transfer to slow cooker stoneware.

2. Cover and cook on **Low** for 8 to 10 hours or on **High** for 4 to 5 hours.

3. When bean mixture is cooked, make rice. In a heavy pot with a tight-fitting lid, combine rice with 4 cups (1 L) water. Cover, bring to a rapid boil, then turn off the heat, leaving the pot on the warm element. Do not lift the lid or move the pot until rice is ready, which will take about 20 minutes.

For convenience, use a bottled roasted red pepper.

To make Fried Plantains to serve 6, heat 2 tbsp (25 mL) vegetable oil or butter over medium heat. Add 4 sliced plantains and cook until browned. Sprinkle with 2 tbsp (25 mL) lemon or lime juice and serve immediately.

If, like me, you particularly enjoy the taste of cumin, toast the cumin seeds and lightly crush them before adding to the mixture. In a large dry skillet, toast cumin seeds until they release their aroma. Transfer to a spice grinder or mortar, or use the bottom of a measuring cup or wine bottle to coarsely grind.

⦿ ⦿ ⦿ ⦿ ⦿

Make ahead

This dish can be prepared the night before it is cooked but without adding the rice, red and green peppers, cilantro, green onions and lemon or lime juice. Complete Step 1 and refrigerate overnight. The next day, continue cooking as directed in Step 2.

4. Meanwhile, add roasted red pepper and green pepper to contents of slow cooker and stir well. Cover and cook on **High** for 20 to 30 minutes, until green pepper is tender.

5. Stir cooked rice into slow cooker. Add lemon or lime juice, cilantro and green onions and stir to combine thoroughly. Serve hot as a main course or cold as a salad.

Split Pea and Lentil Curry with Crispy Onions

SERVES 4 TO 6

• • • • •

I like to serve this tasty Indian-style dish with a cucumber or tomato salad, steamed rice and hot naan, an Indian flat bread. It makes a delicious and nutritious meal.

• • • • •

Tip

Unlike dried beans, lentils do not need to be presoaked. Just remove any that are imperfect and rinse thoroughly under cold water.

• • • • •

Make ahead

This dish can be assembled the night before it is cooked but without adding the Crispy Onion Topping. Complete Steps 1 and 2 and refrigerate overnight. The next day, continue cooking as directed in Step 3. Alternately, curry may be cooked overnight and refrigerated until you're ready to serve. In a Dutch oven, bring to a boil and simmer for 5 to 10 minutes before serving.

1 cup	yellow split peas (chana dal)	250 mL
1 tbsp	vegetable oil	15 mL
1	onion, finely chopped	1
2	cloves garlic, minced	2
1 tbsp	grated gingerroot	15 mL
2 tsp	cumin seeds (see Tips, page 50)	10 mL
1 tsp	coriander seeds	5 mL
1 tsp	mustard seeds	5 mL
1/2 tsp	turmeric	2 mL
1/2 tsp	cayenne pepper	2 mL
1/2 tsp	ground cinnamon	2 mL
1 cup	brown lentils, picked over and rinsed	250 mL
4 cups	vegetable stock	1 L
1 cup	frozen green peas, thawed (optional)	250 mL

CRISPY ONION TOPPING

1 tbsp	clarified butter or vegetable oil	15 mL
2	onions, cut in half vertically, then cut into paper-thin slices	2

1. Soak peas according to either method in Basic Beans (see page 100). Drain and rinse and set aside.

2. In a skillet, heat oil over medium heat. Add onion and cook until soft. Add garlic, gingerroot, cumin seeds, coriander seeds, mustard seeds, turmeric, cayenne and cinnamon and cook, stirring, for 1 minute. Add yellow split peas, lentils and vegetable stock and stir to combine.

3. Transfer mixture to slow cooker stoneware, cover and cook on **Low** for 10 to 12 hours or on **High** for 5 to 6 hours, until peas and lentils are tender. Stir in green peas, if using. Cover and cook on **High** for 15 minutes, until peas are tender.

4. Crispy Onion Topping: In a skillet, heat clarified butter or oil over high heat. Add onions and cook, stirring constantly, until crisp and brown. Ladle curry into individual bowls and top with crispy onions.

Succulent Succotash

SERVES 8 TO 10

• • • • •

Made with freshly picked corn, succotash has become a late summer and autumn tradition. This makes a large batch, but it keeps well.

• • • • •

Tip

This dish works best made with a robust vegetable stock such as Enhanced Vegetable Stock (see recipe, page 38). If you don't have time to make Enhanced Vegetable Stock and you think your stock may be lacking in flavor, add a bit of vegetable bouillon powder, but be aware that you may have to reduce the quantity of salt in the recipe.

• • • • •

Make ahead

This dish can be partially assembled the night before it is cooked. Complete Step 1 and refrigerate overnight. The next day, continue cooking as directed in Step 2. Alternately, succotash can be cooked overnight and refrigerated until you're ready to serve. In a Dutch oven, bring to a boil and simmer for 5 to 10 minutes before serving.

1 tbsp	vegetable oil	15 mL
2	onions, finely chopped	2
4	stalks celery, peeled and thinly sliced	4
2	large carrots, cut in quarters lengthwise, then thinly sliced	2
4	cloves garlic, minced	4
2 tsp	paprika	10 mL
2	sprigs fresh rosemary or 1 tbsp (15 mL) dried rosemary leaves	2
1 tsp	each salt and cracked black peppercorns	5 mL
1	can (28 oz/796 mL) tomatoes, including juice, coarsely chopped (see Tip, page 46)	1
1½ cups	vegetable stock (see Tip, left)	375 mL
4 cups	frozen lima beans, or 2 cups (500 mL) dried lima beans, cooked and drained (see Basic Beans, page 100)	1 L
2 cups	corn kernels	500 mL
1 cup	whipping (35%) cream (optional)	250 mL
	Freshly grated Parmesan cheese (optional)	
	Freshly grated nutmeg, to taste	

1. In a skillet, heat oil over medium heat. Add onions, celery and carrots and cook, stirring, until softened, about 7 minutes. Add garlic, paprika, rosemary, salt and peppercorns and cook, stirring, for 1 minute. Stir in tomatoes with juice and stock and bring to a boil. Place beans and corn in stoneware. Add contents of pan and stir well.

2. Cover and cook on **Low** for 8 to 10 hours or on **High** for 4 to 5 hours, until hot and bubbling. Stir in cream and Parmesan, if using, and season with nutmeg.

Potato-and-Cauliflower Dal with Spicy Shallots

SERVES 6 TO 8

• • • • •

This simple curry, made with yellow split peas, is both hearty and tasty. Stir in the Spicy Shallots so their flavor will disperse throughout.

• • • • •

Make ahead

This dish can be assembled the night before it is cooked but without adding the shallots. Complete Steps 1 and 2 and refrigerate overnight. The next day, continue cooking as directed in Step 3. Alternately, the dal may be cooked overnight and refrigerated until you're ready to serve. In a Dutch oven, bring to a boil and simmer for 5 to 10 minutes before serving.

1 cup	yellow split peas (chana dal)	250 mL
2 tbsp	clarified butter or vegetable oil	25 mL
2	onions, finely chopped	2
4	stalks celery, peeled and thinly sliced	4
4	cloves garlic, minced	4
1 tbsp	minced gingerroot	15 mL
1 tsp	curry powder	5 mL
1 tsp	salt	5 mL
1/2 tsp	cracked black peppercorns	2 mL
1/4 tsp	ground nutmeg	1 mL
3 cups	vegetable stock or water	750 mL
3	potatoes, peeled and cut into 1/2-inch (1 cm) cubes	3
1	small cauliflower, cut into florets, or 4 cups (1 L) frozen cauliflower florets	1

SPICY SHALLOTS

2 tbsp	clarified butter or vegetable oil	25 mL
2	long French shallots, thinly sliced, or 8 green onions, white part only, thinly sliced	2
1/4 to 1/2 tsp	finely chopped chili pepper	1 to 2 mL
1 tbsp	finely chopped cilantro	15 mL
2 tbsp	balsamic vinegar or lemon juice	25 mL

1. Soak peas in 6 cups (1.5 L) water overnight or for 4 hours at room temperature. Drain and rinse and set aside.

2. In a skillet, heat clarified butter or oil over medium heat. Add onions and celery and cook, stirring, until softened, about 5 minutes. Add garlic, gingerroot, curry powder, salt, peppercorns and nutmeg and cook, stirring, for 1 minute. Add vegetable stock or water and bring to a boil. Place potatoes, cauliflower and soaked peas in slow cooker stoneware. Pour onion mixture over and stir well.

3. Cover and cook on **Low** for 10 to 12 hours or on **High** for 5 to 6 hours, until vegetables are tender.

4. Spicy Shallots: In a skillet, heat clarified butter or oil over medium-high heat. Add shallots and cook, stirring, until crisp. Remove pan from heat. Stir in chilies, cilantro and balsamic vinegar or lemon juice. Transfer to a small bowl. Ladle dal into individual bowls, top with Spicy Shallots and stir well.

Cider Baked Beans

SERVES 8

• • • • •

If, like me, you often have small quantities of several varieties of dried beans in your pantry, here is a great way to use them up. For a festive presentation, add the bread crumb or caramelized apple topping. I like to serve this with a salad of shredded carrots and steamed brown bread.

• • • • •

Make ahead

To manage your time most effectively when making this dish, soak the dried beans overnight. Chop and peel the onions, celery, carrots, parsnips and garlic the night before you plan to cook. Cover and refrigerate overnight. Measure the dried spices and cover. Combine apple cider, water and maple syrup in a 4-cup (1 L) measure. Cover and refrigerate overnight. The next morning, drain and rinse the beans and proceed with the recipe.

2 cups	assorted dried beans	500 mL
2	onions, finely chopped	2
3	stalks celery, peeled and thinly sliced	3
2	carrots, peeled and thinly sliced	2
2	large parsnips, peeled and thinly sliced	2
2	cloves garlic, minced	2
2 tsp	chili powder	10 mL
I tsp	salt	5 mL
I tsp	cracked black peppercorns	5 mL
4	whole cloves	4
I	cinnamon stick piece, about 2 inches (5 cm)	I
I cup	apple cider or juice	250 mL
I cup	water	250 mL
½ cup	maple syrup	125 mL
2 tbsp	cornstarch, dissolved in 2 tbsp (25 mL) cold water	25 mL

1. Soak beans according to either method in Basic Beans (see page 100). Drain and rinse and set aside.

2. In slow cooker stoneware, combine beans, onions, celery, carrots, parsnips, garlic, chili powder, salt, peppercorns, cloves, cinnamon, apple cider, water and maple syrup. Cover and cook on **Low** for 10 to 12 hours or on **High** for 5 to 6 hours, until beans are tender.

3. In a bowl, combine dissolved cornstarch with 2 tbsp (25 mL) hot cooking liquid from beans and stir until smooth. Gradually add up to ¼ cup (50 mL) hot bean liquid, stirring until mixture is smooth. Return mixture to stoneware and stir well until sauce thickens.

Variations

Cider Baked Beans with Bread Crumb Topping

Preheat broiler. After beans are cooked, ladle them into individual heatproof tureens or a baking dish. In a bowl, combine 1 cup (250 mL) dry bread crumbs with ¼ cup (50 mL) each melted butter and finely chopped parsley. Sprinkle over beans and place under broiler until topping is lightly browned and beans are bubbling.

Cider Baked Beans with Caramelized Apples

Thanks to Cinda Chavich for this idea. When beans are almost cooked, peel and core 4 apples, then slice them vertically into thin slices. In a skillet, over medium heat, melt 3 tbsp (45 mL) butter. Add ¼ cup (50 mL) brown sugar and cook, stirring, for about 2 minutes. Add apple slices and stir to coat with sugar mixture. Add ¼ cup (50 mL) rum. Increase heat to medium-high and cook, turning, until the liquid evaporates and the apples are tender. Arrange apple slices on top of beans, cover and cook on **High** for 1 hour.

Savory Chickpea Stew with Roasted Red Pepper Coulis

SERVES 6 TO 8

• • • • •

I love this mixture of Mediterranean and Indian flavors, with a Red Pepper Coulis for a contemporary flair.

• • • • •

Tip

The basil adds a nice note to the Coulis, but if you can't get fresh leaves, omit it — the Coulis will be quite tasty, anyway.

• • • • •

Make ahead

This dish can be completely assembled the night before it is cooked except for the Coulis. Complete Step 1 and refrigerate overnight. The next day, continue cooking as directed in Step 2. Alternately, the stew may be cooked overnight and refrigerated until you're ready to serve. In a Dutch oven, bring to a boil and simmer for 5 to 10 minutes before serving.

STEW

2 tsp	cumin seeds	10 mL
I	large eggplant, peeled, cut into 2-inch (5 cm) cubes and drained of excess moisture (see Tip, page 23)	I
I tbsp	vegetable oil	15 mL
I	large onion, finely chopped	I
4	cloves garlic, finely chopped	4
I tsp	dried oregano leaves	5 mL
½ tsp	turmeric	2 mL
I cup	vegetable stock	250 mL
I	can (28 oz/796 mL) tomatoes, including juice, coarsely chopped (see Tip, page 46)	I
2	large potatoes, cut into ½-inch (1 cm) cubes	2
I	can (14 to 19 oz/398 to 540 mL) chickpeas, rinsed and drained, or 1 cup (250 mL) dried chickpeas, cooked and drained (See Basic Beans, page 100)	I

RED PEPPER COULIS

2	roasted red bell peppers (see Tip, page 112)	2
3	oil-packed sun-dried tomatoes, chopped	3
2 tbsp	extra virgin olive oil	25 mL
I tbsp	balsamic vinegar	15 mL
10	fresh basil leaves (optional) (see Tip, left)	10

1. In a skillet, over medium heat, toast cumin seeds until they release their aroma and just begin to turn brown. Transfer to a mortar or a spice grinder and grind coarsely. Set aside.

2. In same skillet, heat oil over medium heat. Add onion and cook until softened, about 3 minutes. Add sweated eggplant and cook until it begins to brown. Add garlic, reserved cumin, oregano and turmeric and cook for 1 minute. Add stock and tomatoes with juices, stirring and breaking up with a spoon. Bring mixture to a boil and cook, stirring, for 1 minute. In slow cooker stoneware, combine potatoes and chickpeas. Pour tomato mixture over and stir to combine.

3. Cover and cook on **Low** for 8 to 10 hours or on **High** for 4 to 5 hours, until potatoes are tender.

4. Red Pepper Coulis: In a food processor, combine roasted peppers, sun-dried tomatoes, oil, balsamic vinegar and basil, if using, and process until smooth.

5. Ladle stew into bowls and top with Coulis.

Poached Eggs on Spicy Lentils

SERVES 4

• • • • •

This delicious combination is a great cold-weather dish. Add the chilies if you prefer a little spice and accompany with warm Indian bread, such as naan, and hot white rice. The Egg and Lentil Curry (see Variation, right) is a great dish for a buffet table or as part of an Indian-themed meal.

• • • • •

Tip

To poach eggs: In a deep skillet, bring about 2 inches (5 cm) lightly salted water to a boil over medium heat. Reduce heat to low. Break eggs into a measuring cup and, holding the cup close to the surface of the water, slip the eggs into the pan. Cook until whites are set and centers are still soft, 3 to 4 minutes. Remove with a slotted spoon.

• • • • •

Make ahead

This dish can be partially assembled in advance. Complete Step 1. Cover and refrigerate overnight. The next morning, continue with Step 2.

1 tbsp	vegetable oil	15 mL
1 ½ cups	finely chopped onions	375 mL
1 tbsp	minced garlic	15 mL
1 tbsp	minced gingerroot	15 mL
1 tsp	ground coriander seeds	5 mL
1 tsp	cumin seeds	5 mL
1 tsp	cracked black peppercorns	5 mL
1 cup	red lentils, rinsed	250 mL
1	can (28 oz/796 mL) tomatoes, including juice, coarsely chopped	1
2 cups	vegetable stock	500 mL
1 cup	coconut milk	250 mL
	Salt	
1	long green chili pepper or 2 Thai birds-eye chilies, finely chopped (optional)	1
4	eggs	4
	Finely chopped parsley (optional)	

1. In a skillet, heat oil over medium heat. Add onions and cook, stirring, until softened, about 3 minutes. Add garlic, gingerroot, coriander seeds, cumin seeds and peppercorns and cook, stirring, for 1 minute. Add lentils, tomatoes with juice and vegetable stock and bring to a boil. Transfer to slow cooker stoneware.

2. Cover and cook on **Low** for 8 hours or on **High** for 4 hours, until lentils are tender and mixture is bubbling. Stir in coconut milk, salt, to taste, and chili pepper, if using. Cover and cook for 20 to 30 minutes until heated through.

3. When ready to serve, ladle into soup bowls and top each serving with a poached egg (see Tip, left). Garnish with parsley, if using.

Variation

Egg and Lentil Curry
Substitute 4 to 6 hard-cooked eggs for the poached. Peel them and cut into halves. Ladle the curry into a serving dish, arrange the eggs on top and garnish.

Lentil Shepherd's Pie

SERVES 6 TO 8

· · · · ·

This flavorful combination is the ultimate comfort food dish. Don't worry if you're serving fewer people —the leftovers taste great reheated.

· · · · ·

Tip

You can use leftover mashed potatoes in this recipe or even prepared mashed potatoes from the supermarket. However, if your potatoes contain milk, don't add the topping mixture to the slow cooker until the mixture has cooked. Spread topping over the hot lentil mixture. Cover and cook on **High** for 30 minutes, until the potatoes are hot and the cheese has melted.

· · · · ·

Make ahead

This recipe can be partially prepared the night before it is cooked. Complete Step 1 and refrigerate overnight. The next day, continue cooking as directed.

I tbsp	vegetable oil	15 mL
2 cups	finely chopped onions	500 mL
4	stalks celery, thinly sliced	4
2	large carrots, peeled and thinly sliced	2
I tbsp	finely chopped garlic	15 mL
I tsp	salt	5 mL
½ tsp	dried thyme leaves	2 mL
½ tsp	cracked black peppercorns	2 mL
I ½ cups	brown or green lentils, rinsed	375 mL
I	can (28 oz/796 mL) tomatoes, including juice, coarsely chopped	I
2 cups	vegetable stock	500 mL

TOPPING

4 cups	mashed potatoes (see Tip, left)	I L
I cup	dry bread crumbs	250 mL
½ cup	shredded Cheddar cheese (optional)	125 mL

1. In a large skillet, heat oil over medium heat. Add onions, celery and carrots and cook, stirring, for 7 minutes, until vegetables are softened. Add garlic, salt, thyme and peppercorns and cook, stirring, for 1 minute. Add lentils and tomatoes with juice and bring to boil. Transfer to slow cooker stoneware and stir in vegetable stock.

2. Topping: In a bowl, combine mashed potatoes and bread crumbs. Mix well. Spread mixture evenly over lentil mixture. Sprinkle cheese over top, if using. Cover and cook on **Low** for 7 to 8 hours or on **High** for 3 to 4 hours, until hot and bubbling.

Black Bean Torta

SERVES 4 TO 6

• • • • •

A torta is a type of layered casserole often made with beans and tortillas. The ingredients can be similar to those used in enchiladas, but a torta is easier to make because you don't have to bother with rolling the tortillas up — just cut into wedges and serve. Pass the sour cream and salsa at the table and, since this is quite rich, add a tossed green salad to lighten up the meal.

• • • • •

Tip

Toast cumin seeds in a large dry skillet until they release their aroma. Transfer to a spice grinder or mortar, or use the bottom of a measuring cup or wine bottle to coarsely grind.

1 tbsp	cumin seeds, toasted and coarsely ground (see Tip, left)	15 mL
1 tbsp	vegetable oil	15 mL
2 cups	chopped onions	500 mL
1 tbsp	minced garlic	15 mL
1 tbsp	dried oregano leaves	15 mL
1 tsp	cracked black peppercorns	5 mL
3 cups	corn kernels	750 mL
1	can (14 to 19 oz/398 to 540 mL) black beans, drained and rinsed, or 1 cup (250 mL) dried black beans, cooked and drained (see Basic Beans, page 100)	1
3 cups	tomato sauce	750 mL
4 oz	cream cheese, cut into cubes	125 g
8	medium flour tortillas	8
1 ½	can (4.5 oz/127 mL) chopped mild green chilies, drained or 2 roasted red peppers, finely chopped	1
1 cup	shredded Monterey Jack cheese	250 mL
	Sour cream	
	Salsa	

1. In a large skillet, heat oil over medium heat. Add onions and cook, stirring, until softened, about 3 minutes. Add garlic, cumin, oregano and peppercorns and cook, stirring for 1 minute. Add corn, black beans and tomato sauce and bring to a boil. Add cream cheese and stir until melted. Remove from heat.

2. Spoon about ½ cup (125 mL) of bean mixture into the bottom of the slow cooker stoneware. Lay 1 tortilla on top of mixture. Spread ½ cup (125 mL) bean mixture over tortilla. Repeat until all the tortillas are used up. Pour remaining sauce over top of the torta. Cover and cook on **Low** for 6 to 8 hours or on **High** for 3 to 4 hours, until mixture is hot and bubbling.

3. Spread green chilies evenly over top of torta and sprinkle evenly with shredded cheese. Cover and cook on **High** for 30 minutes until cheese is melted.

Blue Plate Chili

SERVES 4 TO 6

• • • • •

Here's a good, basic chili recipe — a vegetarian version of the chili my mother used to make or that we ate for lunch at local restaurants when, as a preschooler, I accompanied her on household errands. I have fond memories of those "blue plate specials" of chili and toast, and judging by my own family's response to this version, it remains a popular dish. I still serve it with toast, although whole grain — it wouldn't be the same without it.

• • • • •

Make ahead

This recipe may be partially prepared the night before it is cooked. Chop green pepper, cover and refrigerate. Complete Step 1. Cover and refrigerate overnight. The next morning continue with Step 2.

I tbsp	vegetable oil	15 mL
I	onion, finely chopped	I
4	stalks celery, peeled and thinly sliced	4
4	cloves garlic, minced	4
I tbsp	chili powder	15 mL
I tsp	caraway seeds	5 mL
I tsp	salt	5 mL
I tsp	cracked black peppercorns	5 mL
I	can (28 oz/796 mL) tomatoes, drained and coarsely chopped	I
2 cups	vegetable stock	250 mL
I	can (14 to 19 oz/398 to 540 mL) red kidney beans, drained and rinsed, or I cup (250 mL) dried red kidney beans, soaked, cooked and drained	I
I	green bell pepper, diced	I
I cup	textured vegetable protein	250 mL

1. In a nonstick skillet, heat oil over medium heat. Add onion and celery and cook, stirring, until softened, about 5 minutes. Add garlic, chili powder, caraway seeds, salt and peppercorns and cook, stirring, for 1 minute. Stir in tomatoes and vegetable stock and bring to a boil. Transfer to slow cooker stoneware. Stir in beans.

2. Cover and cook on **Low** for 8 to 10 hours or on **High** for 4 to 5 hours. Increase heat to **High**. Add green pepper and textured vegetable protein and cook for 20 minutes, until pepper is tender.

Indian-Spiced Beans

SERVES 6 TO 8

• • • • •

These tasty beans are great over rice, accompanied by Indian bread and a vegetable or salad of fresh, leafy greens. Add the chili pepper if you like spice, and the cilantro for appearance and flavor.

• • • • •

Make ahead

This dish can be partially prepared the night before it is cooked. Complete Steps 1 and 2. Cover and refrigerate overnight. The next morning continue cooking as directed.

2 tsp	each cumin and coriander seeds	10 mL
1 tbsp	vegetable oil	15 mL
2 cups	finely chopped onions	500 mL
1 tbsp	each minced garlic and gingerroot	15 mL
1 tsp	turmeric	5 mL
1 tsp	salt	5 mL
½ tsp	cracked black peppercorns	2 mL
½ tsp	ground cardamom	2 mL
2	bay leaves	2
1	can (28 oz/796 mL) tomatoes, including juice, coarsely chopped	1
1 cup	vegetable stock	250 mL
3 cups	canned black beans or red kidney beans, rinsed and drained, or 1½ cups (375 mL) dried beans, cooked (see Basic Beans, page 100)	750 mL
1 cup	plain yogurt (optional)	250 mL
1	long red or green or Thai chili pepper, finely chopped (optional)	1
	Finely chopped cilantro (optional)	

1. In a large dry skillet, toast cumin and coriander seeds until they release their aroma. Transfer to a spice grinder or mortar, or use the bottom of a measuring cup or wine bottle to coarsely grind. Set aside.

2. In same skillet, heat oil over medium heat. Add onions and cook, stirring, until softened, about 3 minutes. Add garlic, gingerroot, cumin and coriander seeds, turmeric, salt, peppercorns and cardamom and cook, stirring, for 1 minute. Add bay leaves, tomatoes with juice and vegetable stock and bring to a boil. Place beans in slow cooker stoneware and cover with tomato mixture.

3. Cover and cook on **Low** for 8 to 10 hours or on **High** for 4 to 5 hours, until beans are tender.

4. Stir in yogurt and chili pepper, if using. Garnish with cilantro, if using. Serve immediately.

Smoky White Chili with Potatoes

SERVES 4 TO 6

• • • • •

This delicious white chili, seasoned with a smoky chipotle pepper, has an enticing flavor and soothing texture. Add a sliced tomato or tossed green salad for a tasty and nutritious meal.

• • • • •

Tip

If using, make sure the cream cheese is softened before adding to the slow cooker. Otherwise, it will take a long time to melt.

• • • • •

Make ahead

This dish can be assembled the night before it is cooked. Complete Steps 1 and 2. Cover and refrigerate overnight. The next morning, continue cooking as directed.

2 tsp	cumin seeds	10 mL
1 tbsp	vegetable oil	15 mL
2	onions, finely chopped	2
4	stalks celery, thinly sliced	4
1 tbsp	minced garlic	15 mL
2 tsp	dried oregano leaves	10 mL
1 tsp	cracked black peppercorns	5 mL
1 tsp	salt	5 mL
2	medium potatoes, peeled and cut into 1/2-inch (1 cm) cubes	2
1 cup	white kidney beans, soaked, drained and rinsed	250 mL
4 cups	vegetable stock	1 L
1	chipotle chili in adobo sauce, finely chopped	1
4 oz	cream cheese, cut into 1/2-inch (1 cm) cubes), and softened (optional)	125 g
	Finely chopped cilantro or parsley	

1. In a large dry skillet, toast cumin seeds until they release their aroma. Transfer to a spice grinder or mortar, or use the bottom of a measuring cup or wine bottle to coarsely grind. Set aside.

2. In same skillet, heat oil over medium heat. Add onions and celery and cook, stirring, until vegetables are softened, about 5 minutes. Add garlic, oregano, reserved cumin, peppercorns and salt and cook, stirring, for 1 minute. Place potatoes on bottom of slow cooker. Add beans, stock and onion mixture.

3. Cover and cook on **Low** for 8 hours or on **High** for 4 hours, until potatoes are tender. Add chipotle chili and cream cheese, if using. Stir well. Cover and cook on **High** for 30 minutes, until cheese is melted. Garnish with cilantro or parsley and serve immediately.

Red Beans and Greens

SERVES 6 TO 8

• • • • •

Few meals could be more healthful than this delicious combination of hot leafy greens over flavorful beans. I like to make this with collard greens but other dark leafy greens such as kale work well, too. The smoked paprika makes the dish more robust but it isn't essential. If you're cooking for a smaller group, make the full quantity of beans, spoon off what is needed, and serve with the appropriate quantity of cooked greens. Refrigerate or freeze the leftover beans for another meal.

• • • • •

Make ahead

This dish can be partially prepared the night before it is cooked. Complete Steps 1 and 2. Cover and refrigerate overnight. The next day continue cooking as directed.

2 cups	dried kidney beans	500 mL
1 tbsp	vegetable oil	15 mL
2	large onions, finely chopped	2
2	stalks celery, finely chopped	2
4	cloves garlic, minced	4
1 tsp	dried oregano leaves	5 mL
1 tsp	salt	5 mL
½ tsp	cracked black peppercorns	2 mL
½ tsp	dried thyme leaves	2 mL
¼ tsp	ground allspice or 6 whole allspice, tied in a piece of cheesecloth	1 mL
2	bay leaves	2
4 cups	vegetable stock	1 L
1 tsp	smoked paprika (optional)	5 mL
GREENS		
2 lb	greens, thoroughly washed, stems removed and chopped	1 kg
	Butter or butter substitute	
1 tbsp	balsamic vinegar	15 mL
	Salt and freshly ground black pepper	

1. Soak beans according to either method in Basic Beans (see page 100). Drain and rinse and set aside.

2. In a skillet, heat oil over medium heat. Add onions and celery and cook, stirring, until softened, about 5 minutes. Add garlic, oregano, salt, peppercorns, thyme, allspice and bay leaves and cook, stirring for 1 minute. Transfer to slow cooker stoneware. Add beans and vegetable stock.

3. Cover and cook on **Low** for 8 to 10 hours or on **High** for 4 to 5 hours. Stir in smoked paprika, if using.

4. Greens: Steam greens until tender, about 10 minutes for collards. Toss with butter or butter substitute and balsamic vinegar. Season with salt and pepper to taste. Add to beans and stir to combine. Serve immediately.

Hot Multigrain Cereal *page 142* ➤
Overleaf: New Potato Curry *page 150*

Tomato Dal with Spinach

SERVES 4 TO 6

• • • • •

This mildly-spiced but tasty dal is delicious over hot cooked rice or as a substantial side dish. Add the yogurt, if you prefer a creamy finish.

• • • • •

Tips

Split yellow peas take a long time to cook and in my experience, need to be soaked before cooking. I recommend soaking this quantity in 8 cups (2 L) of water overnight or for 4 hours at room temperature. Drain and rinse before using in this recipe.

If you have leftover baby spinach for salad you can substitute it for the regular spinach in this recipe. About half of a (10 oz/284 g) bag is an appropriate quantity as unlike regular spinach, there is no waste.

If you prefer, substitute 2 parsnips for 2 of the carrots.

• • • • •

Make ahead

This dish can be partially prepared the night before it is cooked. Complete Steps 1, 2 and 3. Cover and refrigerate overnight. The next day continue cooking as directed.

2 cups	yellow split peas (see Tips, left)	500 mL
2 tsp	cumin seeds	10 mL
1 tsp	whole coriander seeds	5 mL
1 tbsp	vegetable oil	15 mL
1	medium onion, finely chopped	1
6	carrots, peeled and diced	6
6	cloves garlic, finely chopped	6
1 tbsp	minced gingerroot	15 mL
1 tsp	salt	5 mL
½ tsp	cracked black peppercorns	2 mL
1	can (28 oz/796 mL) tomatoes, including juice, coarsely chopped	1
2 cups	vegetable stock	500 mL
8 oz	fresh spinach leaves, washed or 1 package (10 oz/300 g) frozen spinach, thawed (see Tips, left)	250 g
1 tbsp	freshly squeezed lemon juice	15 mL
	Plain yogurt (optional)	

1. Soak peas in 8 cups (2 L) water overnight or for 4 hours at room temperature. Drain and rinse and set aside.

2. In a dry skillet, toast cumin and coriander seeds until they release their aroma. Transfer to a spice grinder or mortar, or use the bottom of a measuring cup or wine bottle to coarsely grind. Set aside.

3. In same skillet, heat oil over medium heat. Add onion and carrots and cook, stirring, until softened, about 7 minutes. Add garlic, gingerroot, salt and peppercorns and cook, stirring for 1 minute. Add tomatoes with juice and bring to a boil, breaking up with a spoon. Transfer to slow cooker stoneware. Add vegetable stock and yellow split peas and stir to combine.

4. Cover and cook on **Low** for 10 to 12 hours or on **High** for 4 to 5 hours, until peas are soft. Add spinach and lemon juice. Cover and cook on **High** for 20 minutes until spinach is cooked and mixture is bubbling. Ladle into bowls and drizzle with yogurt, if using.

◄ Rice Pudding with Cherries and Almonds *page 158*
Overleaf: Leeks à la Greque *page 152*

Hominy and Red Bean Chili

SERVES 6 TO 8

• • • • •

This tasty chili is brimming with flavorful vegetables. For a change, try finishing with Avocado Topping (see Tips, below) instead of the usual fixings.

• • • • •

Tips

Use any red bean such as small red Mexican beans, kidney beans or even pink pinto beans in this recipe.

To make Avocado Topping: In a bowl, combine 2 tbsp (25 mL) each finely chopped green onion and cilantro. Add 1 tbsp (15 mL) lime juice and 1 avocado, chopped into ½-inch (1 cm) cubes. Toss to combine. This topping makes a nice finish for many chilies.

For convenience, use frozen diced squash in this recipe.

• • • • •

Make ahead

This dish can be assembled before it is cooked, without adding the chipotle chilies. Complete Steps 1 and 2. Cover and refrigerate. When you are ready to cook, continue with Step 3.

2 tsp	cumin seeds	10 mL
4	whole allspice	4
1 tbsp	vegetable oil	15 mL
2	onions, finely chopped	2
2	carrots, peeled and chopped	2
4	cloves garlic, minced	4
1 tsp	chili powder	5 mL
1 tsp	dried oregano leaves	5 mL
1	can (28 oz/796 mL) tomatoes, including juice, coarsely chopped	1
1 cup	vegetable stock	250 mL
1	can (14 to 19 oz/398 to 540 mL) red kidney beans, drained and rinsed or 1 cup (250 mL) dried red kidney beans, cooked and drained (see Basic Beans, page 100)	1
1	can (15 oz/475 mL) hominy, drained and rinsed	1
2 cups	cubed (½ inch/1 cm) peeled celery root	500 mL
2 cups	diced yellow squash (see Tips, left)	500 mL
1 to 2	chipotle chilies in adobo sauce, finely chopped	1 to 2
	Shredded lettuce (optional)	
	Finely chopped green onion (optional)	
	Finely chopped cilantro	
	Sour cream (optional)	

1. In a large dry skillet, toast cumin seeds and allspice, stirring, until they release their aroma. Transfer to a spice grinder or mortar, or use the bottom of a measuring cup or wine bottle to coarsely grind. Set aside.

2. In same skillet, heat oil over medium heat. Add onions and carrots and cook, stirring, until carrots are softened, about 7 minutes. Add garlic, chili powder, oregano and reserved cumin and allspice and cook, stirring for 1 minute. Add tomatoes with juice and vegetable stock and bring to a boil. Transfer to slow cooker stoneware. Add beans, hominy, celery root and squash and stir to combine.

3. Cover and cook on **Low** for 8 hours or on **High** for 4 hours, until vegetables are tender. Stir in chipotle chilies. Cover and cook on **High** for 15 minutes, to blend flavors. Ladle into bowls and garnish with shredded lettuce and green onion, if using, and cilantro. Top each serving with a dollop of sour cream, if using.

Variation

Hominy and Chickpea Chili
Substitute an equal quantity of chickpeas for the beans.

Cashew Lentil Loaf

SERVES 6

• • • • •

Shredded carrots and red pepper add a burst of color to this tasty loaf, which is also good served cold.

• • • • •

Tip

Use 1 can (14 to 19 oz/398 to 540 mL) green or brown lentils, drained and rinsed.

• • • • •

Make ahead

This loaf can be partially prepared before it is cooked. Complete Steps 1, 2 and 3. Refrigerate overnight. The next day, continue with Step 4.

I tbsp	cumin seeds	15 mL
I tbsp	vegetable oil	15 mL
I	large onion, finely chopped	I
2	stalks celery, diced	2
2 cups	shredded carrots	500 mL
2	cloves garlic, minced	2
I	red bell pepper, diced	I
½ to I	long red or green chili pepper, diced	½ to I
I tsp	salt	5 mL
½ tsp	cracked black peppercorns	2 mL
2 cups	cooked green or brown lentils, drained and rinsed (see Tip, left)	500 mL
3 cups	shredded Cheddar cheese	750 mL
I cup	coarsely chopped cashews	250 mL
3	eggs, beaten	3

1. In a large dry skillet, over medium heat, toast cumin seeds until they begin to brown and release their aroma. Immediately transfer to a mortar or spice grinder and grind to a powder. Set aside.

2. Return skillet to element and heat oil. Add onion and celery and cook, stirring, until celery softens, about 5 minutes. Add carrots, garlic, red pepper, chili pepper, salt and peppercorns and cook, stirring for 2 minutes. Remove from heat and set aside.

3. In a large mixing bowl, combine lentils, cheese and cashews. Add contents of skillet and stir well. Add eggs and mix until blended. Spoon into prepared pan and cover tightly with foil, securing with a string.

4. Place in slow cooker stoneware and pour in enough boiling water to come 1 inch (2.5 cm) up the sides. Cover and cook on **High** for 4 to 5 hours, until loaf has set.

Mushroom Cholent

SERVES 8

• • • • •

Cholent made with brisket, which is prepared on Friday and left to cook overnight, is the traditional midday meal for the Jewish Sabbath. In this version, portobello mushrooms provide heartiness and a *mirepoix* containing parsnips, as well as the traditional vegetables, adds sweetness and flavor. The mushrooms contribute to a surprisingly rich gravy and the results are very good indeed.

• • • • •

Tip

Although traditional wisdom holds that adding salt to dried beans before they are cooked will make them tough, when food scientist Shirley Corriher actually tested this premise she found the opposite to be true. Adding salt to beans while they cooked produced a more tender result.

• • • • •

Make ahead

This dish can be assembled before it is cooked. Complete Steps 1 and 2. Cover and refrigerate. When you are ready to cook, continue with Step 3.

I cup	dried white navy beans	250 mL
I tbsp	vegetable oil	15 mL
2	onions, finely chopped	2
4	stalks celery, diced	4
2	carrots, peeled and diced	2
2	parsnips, peeled and diced	2
6	cloves garlic, minced	6
I tbsp	minced gingerroot	15 mL
2 tsp	paprika	10 mL
I tsp	salt	5 mL
I tsp	cracked black peppercorns	5 mL
4 cups	vegetable stock	I L
2	potatoes, peeled and cut into ½-inch (1 cm) cubes	2
12 oz	portobello mushroom caps (about 4 large)	375 g
I cup	pearl barley, rinsed	250 mL

1. Soak beans according to either method in Basic Beans (see page 100). Drain and rinse and set aside.

2. In a skillet, heat oil over medium heat. Add onions, celery, carrots and parsnips and cook, stirring, until softened, about 7 minutes. Add garlic, gingerroot, paprika, salt and peppercorns and cook, stirring for 1 minute. Stir in vegetable stock and remove from heat.

3. Pour half the contents of pan into slow cooker stoneware. Set remainder aside. Spread potatoes evenly over mixture. Arrange mushrooms evenly over potatoes, cutting one to fit, if necessary. Spread barley and reserved beans evenly over mushrooms. Add remaining onion mixture to stoneware.

4. Cover and cook on **Low** for 10 to 12 hours, or on **High** for 5 to 6 hours until beans are tender.

Tamale Pie with Chili Cornmeal Crust

SERVES 6 TO 8

• • • • •

This hearty and flavorful dish makes a terrific potluck dish, or a centerpiece for a buffet table. All it needs is a tossed salad and ice-cold beer.

• • • • •

Make ahead

This dish can be assembled the night before it is cooked. Complete Steps 1 and 2. Cover and refrigerate overnight. The next morning, continue with Step 3.

1 tbsp	cumin seeds	15 mL
1 tbsp	vegetable oil	15 mL
2	onions, finely chopped	2
2	carrots, peeled and diced	2
2	stalks celery, diced	2
1 tbsp	chili powder	15 mL
1 tbsp	dried oregano leaves	15 mL
1 tsp	salt	5 mL
1/2 tsp	cracked black peppercorns	2 mL
1 cup	ketchup	250 mL
1	can (14 oz/398 mL) refried beans	1
1	can (14 to 19 oz/398 to 540 mL) black beans, drained and rinsed, or 1 cup (250 mL) dried black beans, cooked and drained (see Basic Beans, page 100)	1
1 cup	vegetable stock	250 mL
2 cups	corn kernels	500 mL

CORNMEAL TOPPING

1 cup	cornmeal	250 mL
1/2 cup	all-purpose flour	125 mL
2 tsp	baking powder	10 mL
1/2 tsp	salt	2 mL
1/4 tsp	freshly ground black pepper	1 mL
1 cup	milk	250 mL
1/4 cup	melted butter	50 mL
1	egg, beaten	1
1 cup	shredded Monterey Jack cheese	250 mL
1	can (4.5 oz/127 mL) chopped mild green chilies, including juice	1

1. In a large dry skillet, over medium heat, toast cumin seeds until they begin to brown and release their aroma. Immediately transfer to a mortar or spice grinder and grind to a powder. Set aside.

2. In a skillet, heat oil over medium heat. Add onions, carrots and celery and cook, stirring, until softened, about 7 minutes. Add chili powder, reserved cumin, oregano, salt and peppercorns and cook, stirring, for 1 minute. Stir in ketchup, refried beans and black beans, breaking refried beans up with a spoon until they are fully integrated into the mixture. Add stock and corn and bring to a boil. Transfer to slow cooker stoneware.

3. Cover and cook on **Low** for 6 hours or on **High** for 3 hours, until mixture is bubbling and hot. If cooking on **Low**, increase heat to **High**.

4. Cornmeal Topping: In a bowl, mix together cornmeal, flour, baking powder, salt and pepper. Make a well in the center. Add milk, butter and egg and mix until just blended with dry ingredients. Stir in cheese and chilies with juice. Spread mixture evenly over filling. Place two clean tea towels, each folded in half (so you will have four layers) over top of stoneware to absorb the moisture generated during cooking. Cover and cook on **High** for 1 hour until the top is risen and crusty.

Mediterranean White Beans

SERVES 6

• • • • •

Serve this dish accompanied by a tossed green or sliced tomato salad. For a great finishing touch, top each serving with Toasted Bread Crumbs (see Variation, right). In addition to adding texture and flavor to many casseroles and stews, Toasted Bread Crumbs are a great way to use up day-old bread. Try them with other recipes in this book such as Tuscan-Style Beans with Rosemary (page 109) or Braised Fennel with Parsnips (page 92)

• • • • •

Make ahead

This dish can be assembled the night before it is cooked. Complete Steps 1 and 2. Cover and refrigerate overnight. The next morning, continue with Step 3.

1 cup	dried white kidney beans	250 mL
1 tbsp	vegetable oil	15 mL
1	onion, finely chopped	1
2	carrots, peeled and diced	2
4	stalks celery, diced	4
5	cloves garlic, minced	5
2 tsp	dried Italian seasoning	10 mL
1 tsp	salt	5 mL
1/2 tsp	cracked black peppercorns	2 mL
2 1/2 cups	vegetable stock (approx.)	625 mL
2	red bell peppers, roasted, peeled and cut into thin strips	2
20	pitted black olives, thinly sliced	20

1. Soak beans according to either method in Basic Beans (see page 100). Drain and rinse and set aside.

2. In a skillet, heat oil over medium heat. Add onion, carrots and celery and cook, stirring, until vegetables are softened, about 7 minutes. Add garlic, Italian seasoning, salt and peppercorns and cook, stirring, for 1 minute. Transfer mixture to slow cooker stoneware. Add beans and vegetable stock to cover.

3. Cover and cook on **Low** for 8 to 10 hours or on **High** for 4 to 5 hours, until beans are tender. Stir in roasted peppers and olives. Ladle into individual bowls.

Variation
Toasted Bread Crumbs

For 2 cups (500 mL) of bread crumbs, use about 3 slices of a large loaf, each about 1-inch (2.5 cm) thick. Cut each slice into quarters and process in a food processor, fitted with a metal blade, until the crumbs are the size of split peas, about 40 seconds. Add 1/4 tsp (1 mL) each salt and freshly ground black pepper and pulse to combine. In a skillet over medium heat, melt 3 tbsp (45 mL) butter. If you prefer garlic flavor, add 1 tbsp (15 mL) minced garlic and cook, stirring, for 1 minute. Add the bread crumbs and cook, stirring frequently, until evenly browned.

Lentil Sloppy Joes

SERVES 4

• • • • •

Here's a kids' favorite that grown-ups enjoy, too. It makes a great dinner for those busy nights when everyone is coming and going at different times. Leave the slow cooker on Low or Warm, the buns on the counter, the fixins' of salad in the fridge and let everyone help themselves.

• • • • •

Tip

Use 1 can (14 to 19 oz/398 to 540 mL) green or brown lentils, drained and rinsed.

• • • • •

Make ahead

This dish can be assembled the night before it is cooked. Complete Step 1. Cover and refrigerate overnight. The next morning, continue with Step 2.

1 tbsp	vegetable oil	15 mL
1	onion, finely chopped	1
4	stalks celery, diced	4
4	cloves garlic, minced	4
½ tsp	dried oregano leaves	2 mL
½ tsp	salt	2 mL
	Freshly ground black pepper, to taste	
½ cup	tomato ketchup	125 mL
¼ cup	water	50 mL
1 tbsp	balsamic vinegar	15 mL
1 tbsp	brown sugar	15 mL
1 tbsp	Dijon mustard	15 mL
2 cups	cooked brown or green lentils, drained and rinsed (see Tip, left)	500 mL
	Hot pepper sauce (optional)	
	Toasted hamburger buns	

1. In a skillet, heat oil over medium heat. Add onion and celery and cook, stirring, until softened, about 5 minutes. Add garlic, oregano, salt and pepper and cook, stirring for 1 minute. Stir in ketchup, water, balsamic vinegar, brown sugar and mustard. Transfer to slow cooker stoneware. Add lentils and stir well.

2. Cover and cook on **Low** for 6 hours or on **High** for 3 hours, until hot and bubbling. Add hot pepper sauce to taste, if using. Ladle over hot toasted buns and serve immediately.

Chili with Grits Crust

SERVES 6 TO 8

• • • • •

Everyone loves this savory chili with the unusual grits crust. It is a great dish to wind down with, after a day of enjoying the great outdoors. All it needs is a big salad and some robust wine.

• • • • •

Tips

For a change or if you don't like grits, try baking this chili with the Cornmeal Topping (see recipe, page 135).

For convenience, use frozen diced squash

• • • • •

Make ahead

This dish can be assembled the night before it is cooked. Complete Step 1. Cover and refrigerate overnight. The next morning, continue with Step 2.

CHILI

1 tbsp	cumin seeds	15 mL
1 tbsp	vegetable oil	15 mL
2	onions, finely chopped	2
4	cloves garlic, minced	4
1 tbsp	dried oregano leaves	15 mL
1 tbsp	chili powder	15 mL
1 tsp	salt	5 mL
1 tsp	cracked black peppercorns	5 mL
1 tbsp	balsamic vinegar	15 mL
1 tbsp	packed brown sugar	15 mL
1	can (28 oz/796 mL) tomatoes, including juice, coarsely chopped	1
2 cups	vegetable stock	500 mL
4 cups	diced acorn or butternut squash	1 L
2 cups	corn kernels, thawed if frozen	500 mL
1	can (14 to 19 oz/398 to 540 mL) kidney beans, drained and rinsed, or 1 cup (250 mL) dried kidney beans, soaked, cooked and drained (see Basic Beans, page 100)	1
1	green bell pepper, diced	1

CRUST

2½ cups	milk or water	625 mL
¼ tsp	salt	1 mL
1 cup	grits (not quick-cooking)	250 mL
2 tbsp	butter	25 mL
2 tsp	baking powder	10 mL
1	egg, beaten	1
1 cup	shredded Cheddar Cheese	250 mL
1	chipotle chili in adobo sauce, finely chopped (optional)	1

1. In a dry skillet, over medium heat, toast cumin seeds until they release their aroma and just begin to turn brown. Transfer to a mortar or a spice grinder and grind coarsely. Set aside.

2. In same skillet, heat oil over medium heat. Add onions and cook, stirring, until softened, about 3 minutes. Add garlic, reserved cumin, oregano, chili powder, salt and peppercorns and cook, stirring, for 1 minute. Add balsamic vinegar, brown sugar, tomatoes with juice and vegetable stock and stir well. Transfer to slow cooker stoneware. Add squash, corn and kidney beans and stir to blend.

3. Cover and cook on **Low** for 8 hours or on **High** for 4 hours, until hot and bubbling. If cooking on **Low**, increase to **High** before adding green pepper and crust.

4. Crust: In a large saucepan, over medium heat, bring milk or water to a boil. Stir in salt. Gradually stir in grits. Cook, stirring constantly, until mixture is very thick. Remove from heat. Stir in butter, baking powder, egg, cheese and chili, if using. Spread evenly over chili mixture. Place two clean tea towels, each folded in half (so you will have four layers) across the top of the slow cooker stoneware to absorb the moisture generated during cooking. Cover and cook on **High** for $1\frac{1}{4}$ hours until the top is risen and crusty.

Gingery Chickpeas in Spicy Tomato Gravy

SERVES 6 TO 8

• • • • •

This zesty stew can be served as a main course or as a rich side dish. At our house, we like to eat it with hot naan or pita bread and a cool cucumber salad.

• • • • •

Tip

If using canned tomatoes, drain them thoroughly before chopping.

• • • • •

Make ahead

This dish can be completely assembled the night before it is cooked. Complete Step 1 and refrigerate overnight. The next day, continue cooking as directed in Step 2.

1 tbsp	vegetable oil	15 mL
2	onions, finely chopped	2
4	cloves garlic, finely chopped	4
2 tbsp	minced gingerroot	25 mL
2 tsp	ground coriander	10 mL
1 tsp	cumin seeds	5 mL
1 tsp	salt	5 mL
½ tsp	cracked black peppercorns	2 mL
2 tsp	balsamic vinegar	10 mL
2 cups	coarsely chopped tomatoes, canned or fresh	500 mL
2	cans (each 14 to 19 oz/398 to 540 mL) chickpeas, rinsed and drained, or 2 cups (500 mL) dried chickpeas, cooked and drained (see Basic Beans, page 100)	2
	Chopped green onion (optional)	

1. In a skillet, heat oil over medium heat. Add onions and cook, stirring, until they begin to brown, about 10 minutes. Add garlic, gingerroot, coriander, cumin seeds, salt and peppercorns and cook, stirring, for 1 minute. Add balsamic vinegar and tomatoes and bring to a boil. Place chickpeas in slow cooker stoneware. Pour tomato mixture over and stir well.

2. Cover and cook on **Low** for 6 to 8 hours or on **High** for 3 to 4 hours, until hot and bubbling. Garnish with chopped green onion, if using.

Grains and Sides

Hot Breakfast Cereals

SERVES 4

• • • • •

Hot cereal is one of my favorite ways to begin the day, and happily you can use your slow cooker to ensure that all family members get off to a nutritious start. Cook the cereal overnight and turn the slow cooker to Warm in the morning. Everyone can help themselves according to their schedules.

• • • • •

Tips

Multigrain cereals are one way of ensuring that you maximize the nutritional benefits of cereal grains. You can buy them pre-packaged, usually in 3, 5 or 7-grain combinations or under a brand name, or you can make your own by combining your favorite grains. Store multigrain cereal in an airtight container in a cool, dry place.

Rolled oats, often called porridge when cooked, are probably the most popular breakfast cereal. For variety, try the variations called steel-cut oats, Irish oatmeal or Scotch oats, which have an appealing chewy texture.

• These recipes work best in a small (maximum 3½ quart) slow cooker
• Well-greased slow cooker stoneware

Hot Multigrain Cereal

I cup	multigrain cereal, or ½ cup (125 mL) multigrain cereal and ½ cup (125 mL) rolled oats	250 mL
¼ tsp	salt	I mL
4 cups	water	I L
2	medium all-purpose apples, peeled and thickly sliced	2
¼ to ⅓ cup	raisins (optional)	50 to 75 mL

1. In prepared slow cooker stoneware, combine cereal, salt, water and apples. Cover and cook on **Low** for 8 hours or overnight. Just before serving, place raisins, if using, in a microwave-safe bowl and cover with water. Microwave for 20 seconds to soften. Add to hot cereal. Stir well and serve.

Hot Oatmeal

I¼ cups	rolled or steel-cut oats	300 mL
½ tsp	salt	2 mL
4 cups	water	I L

1. In prepared slow cooker stoneware, combine oats, salt and water. Cover and cook on **Low** for 8 hours or overnight. Stir well and serve.

Slow-Cooked Polenta

SERVES 6

• • • • •

Polenta, an extremely versatile dish from northern Italy, is basically cornmeal cooked in seasoned liquid. It is one of my favorite grains. Depending upon the method used, making polenta can be a laborious process. These slow-cooked versions produce excellent results with a minimum of effort.

• • • • •

Tip

You can cook polenta directly in the slow cooker stoneware or in a 6-cup (1.5 L) baking dish, lightly greased, depending upon your preference. If you are cooking directly in the stoneware, I recommend using a small (maximum 3½ quart) slow cooker, lightly greased. If you are using a baking dish, you will need a large (minimum 5 quart) oval slow cooker.

3¾ cups	vegetable stock or water	925 mL
I tsp	salt	5 mL
¼ tsp	freshly ground black pepper	I mL
I¼ cups	cornmeal	300 mL

1. In a saucepan, bring stock, salt and pepper to a boil over medium heat. Add cornmeal in a thin stream, stirring constantly.

2. Direct method: Transfer mixture to prepared slow cooker stoneware (see Tip, left). Cover and cook on **Low** for 1½ hours.

3. Baking dish method: Transfer mixture to prepared baking dish (see Tip, left). Cover with foil and secure with a string. Place dish in slow cooker stoneware and pour in enough boiling water to come 1 inch (2.5 cm) up the sides of the bowl. Cover and cook on **Low** for 1½ hours.

Variation

Creamy Polenta

Substitute 2 cups (500 mL) milk or cream and 1¼ cups (300 mL) stock for the quantity of liquid above. If desired, stir in ¼ cup (50 mL) finely chopped fresh parsley and/or 2 tbsp (25 mL) freshly grated Parmesan cheese, after the cornmeal has been added to the liquid.

Grits 'n' Cheddar Cheese

SERVES 4

• • • • •

I think I must have lived in the American South in a previous life because I'm absolutely crazy about grits. I could eat them for breakfast, lunch and dinner, which is unfortunate, because they can be difficult to find north of the Mason-Dixon Line. They make a great accompaniment to many dishes, embellished with cheese or on their own (see Variation, right).

• Lightly greased slow cooker stoneware
• Works best in a small (3½ quart) slow cooker

2 cups	water	500 mL
1 tbsp	butter	15 mL
1 tsp	salt	5 mL
½ tsp	freshly ground black pepper	2 mL
½ cup	grits (not instant)	125 mL
1 cup	milk	250 mL
2	eggs, beaten	2
1 cup	shredded Cheddar cheese	250 mL

1. In a saucepan, bring water, butter, salt and pepper to a boil over medium heat. Gradually add grits, stirring until smooth.

2. Remove from heat. Add milk, eggs and cheese and stir to blend. Transfer to prepared stoneware. Cover and cook on **High** for 4 hours, until set. Serve immediately.

Variation

Plain Ole Grits

Omit the milk, eggs and cheese. Complete Step 1, using 1 cup (250 mL) stone-ground grits, and 4 cups (1 L) water or vegetable stock. Cover and cook on **Low** for 8 hours or on **High** for 4 hours.

Steamed Brown Bread

**MAKES 1 LARGE
LOAF OR UP TO
3 SMALL LOAVES**

• • • • •

Served warm, this slightly
sweet bread is a delicious
accompaniment to baked
beans. It also goes well with
wedges of Cheddar cheese.

- Three 19-oz (540 mL) vegetable tins, washed, dried and
  sprayed with vegetable oil spray, or one 8-cup (2 L) lightly
  greased soufflé or baking dish
- Large (minimum 5 quart) oval slow cooker

1 cup	all-purpose flour	250 mL
1 cup	whole wheat flour	250 mL
½ cup	rye flour	125 mL
½ cup	cornmeal	125 mL
2 tbsp	granulated sugar	25 mL
1 tsp	salt	5 mL
1 tsp	baking soda	5 mL
1½ cups	buttermilk	375 mL
½ cup	molasses	125 mL
2 tbsp	olive oil	25 mL

1. In a bowl, mix together all–purpose, whole wheat and
rye flours, cornmeal, sugar, salt and baking soda. Make
a well in the center.

2. In a separate bowl, mix together buttermilk, molasses
and olive oil. Pour into well and mix until blended.

3. Spoon batter into prepared cans (in equal amounts)
or baking dish. Cover top(s) with foil and secure with
a string. Place in slow cooker stoneware and pour in
enough boiling water to come 1 inch (2.5 cm) up the
sides of the dish. Cover and cook on **High** for 2 hours,
if using cans, or 3 hours if using a baking dish. Unmold
and serve warm.

Leeks Gratin

SERVES 4 TO 6

· · · · ·

This is an absolutely delicious side dish. I could eat it with just about anything.

· · · · ·

Tip

I have suggested softening the leeks in the slow cooker stoneware to reduce clean up. If time is a greater concern, by all means do this on the stovetop. Melt the butter in a skillet over medium heat. Add the leeks and cook, stirring, until softened, about 5 minutes. Transfer to the stoneware and continue cooking as directed.

8	medium leeks, white and light green part only, split lengthwise, cleaned and cut in half on the horizontal (see Tip, left)	8
2 tbsp	melted butter	25 mL
½ cup	vegetable stock	125 mL
½ cup	shredded Fontina cheese	125 mL
¼ cup	whipping (35%) cream	50 mL
	Salt and freshly ground black pepper, to taste	

1. In slow cooker stoneware, combine leeks and melted butter. Stir to thoroughly coat leeks. Cover and cook on **High** for 30 minutes until leeks are softened. Stir well. Add stock.

2. Cover and cook on **Low** for 6 hours or on **High** for 3 hours, until leeks are tender. Stir in cheese and cream. Cover and cook on **High** for 15 minutes, until cheese is melted and mixture is hot and bubbling. Season with salt and pepper and serve.

New Orleans Braised Onions

SERVES 8 TO 10

• • • • •

I call these New Orleans onions because I was inspired by an old Creole recipe for Spanish onions. In that version, the onions are braised in beef broth enhanced by the addition of liquor such as bourbon or port. After the onions are cooked, the cooking juices are reduced and herbs, such as capers or fresh thyme leaves, may be added to the concentrated sauce. In my opinion, this simplified version is every bit as tasty. Pass the hot pepper sauce at the table, if your guests like spice.

2 to 3	large Spanish onions	2 to 3
6 to 9	whole cloves	6 to 9
1/2 tsp	salt	2 mL
1/2 tsp	cracked black peppercorns	2 mL
Pinch	ground thyme	Pinch
	Grated zest and juice of 1 orange	
1/2 cup	vegetable stock	125 mL
	Finely chopped fresh parsley (optional)	
	Hot pepper sauce (optional)	

1. Stud onions with cloves. Place in slow cooker stoneware and sprinkle with salt, peppercorns, thyme and orange zest. Pour orange juice and vegetable stock over onions, cover and cook on **Low** for 8 hours or on **High** for 4 hours, until onions are tender.

2. Keep onions warm. In a saucepan over medium heat, reduce cooking liquid by half.

3. When ready to serve, cut onions into quarters. Place on a deep platter and cover with sauce. Sprinkle with parsley, if using, and pass the hot pepper sauce, if desired.

Cumin Beets

SERVES 4 TO 6

• • • • •

I love the simple, but unusual and effective combination of flavors in this dish, which is inspired by Indian cuisine. It's my favorite way of cooking small summer beets, fresh from the garden, because I don't have to heat up my kitchen with a pot of simmering water on the stovetop. If you prefer a spicy dish, add hot pepper sauce, to taste, after the beets have finished cooking.

• • • • •

Tip

Peeling the beets before they are cooked ensures that all the delicious cooking juices end up on your plate.

• • • • •

Make ahead

This dish can be assembled the night before it is cooked. Complete Step 1, add beets to mixture and refrigerate overnight. The next day, continue cooking as directed in Step 2.

1 tbsp	vegetable oil	15 mL
1	onion, finely chopped	1
3	cloves garlic, minced	3
1 tsp	cumin seeds	5 mL
1 tsp	salt	5 mL
½ tsp	freshly ground black pepper	2 mL
2	medium tomatoes, peeled and coarsely chopped	2
1 cup	water	250 mL
1 lb	beets, peeled and used whole, if small, or sliced thinly (see Tip, left)	500 g

1. In a skillet, heat oil over medium-high heat. Add onion and cook, stirring, until softened. Stir in garlic, cumin, salt and pepper and cook for 1 minute. Add tomatoes and water and bring to a boil.

2. Place beets in slow cooker stoneware and pour tomato mixture over them. Cover and cook on **Low** for 8 to 10 hours or on **High** for 4 to 5 hours, until beets are tender.

Braised Beets with Sour Cream and Horseradish

SERVES 6 TO 8

• • • • •

This recipe is so good I don't need an excuse to make it.

• • • • •

Make ahead

This dish can be partially prepared the night before it is cooked. Complete Step 1 and refrigerate overnight. The next day, continue cooking as directed in Steps 2 and 3.

6	medium beets, peeled and quartered (see Tip, page 148)	6
2 tbsp	granulated sugar	25 mL
1/4 tsp	salt	1 mL
1/4 tsp	freshly ground black pepper	1 mL
1 tbsp	red wine vinegar	15 mL
2 tbsp	water	25 mL
1/4 cup	sour cream	50 mL
1 tbsp	prepared horseradish	15 mL
	Finely chopped parsley or dill	

1. In slow cooker stoneware, combine beets, sugar, salt, pepper, vinegar and water. Stir well.

2. Cover and cook on **Low** for 8 to 10 hours or on **High** for 4 to 5 hours, until beets are tender.

3. In a small bowl, combine sour cream and horseradish. Toss with beets. Transfer mixture to a serving dish and garnish with parsley or dill.

Variation

Braised Beets with Creamy Horseradish

Substitute 1/4 cup (50 mL) whipping (35%) cream for the sour cream and add 2 tsp (10 mL) sherry wine vinegar along with the horseradish. Garnish with parsley rather than dill.

New Potato Curry

SERVES 4 TO 6

• • • • •

This is an excellent way to cook new potatoes, as they cook slowly, almost in their own juices, in a curry-flavored sauce. It's a great side dish, but you can also serve it as a main course along with a bowl of dal and a green vegetable. It also makes a delicious summer meal, accompanied by a garden salad.

• • • • •

Tip

Leave the skins on potatoes, scrub thoroughly and dry on paper towels. Cut in half any that are larger than 1 inch (2.5 cm) in diameter.

• • • • •

Make ahead

This dish can be partially prepared the night before it is cooked. Complete Steps 1 and 2 and refrigerate overnight. The next day, continue cooking as directed in Step 3.

2 tbsp	clarified butter or vegetable oil	25 mL
I lb	small new potatoes, about 10 new potatoes (see Tip, left)	500 g
2	onions, finely chopped	2
I	clove garlic, minced	I
I tsp	curry powder, preferably Madras	5 mL
½ tsp	salt	2 mL
½ tsp	cracked black peppercorns	2 mL
½ cup	water or vegetable stock	125 mL
2 tbsp	freshly squeezed lemon juice	25 mL
¼ cup	finely chopped cilantro	50 mL

1. In a skillet, heat butter or oil over medium–high heat. Add potatoes and cook just until they begin to brown. Transfer to slow cooker stoneware.

2. Reduce heat to medium. Add onions and cook, stirring, until softened. Add garlic, curry powder, salt and peppercorns. Stir and cook for 1 minute. Add water or stock, bring to a boil and pour over potatoes.

3. Cover and cook on **Low** for 8 hours or on **High** for 4 hours, until potatoes are tender. Stir in lemon juice and garnish with cilantro.

Braised Carrots with Capers

SERVES 4 TO 6

• • • • •

This dish is simplicity itself and yet the results are startlingly fresh.

• • • • •

Make ahead

This dish can be partially prepared the night before it is cooked. Complete Step 1 and refrigerate overnight. The next day, continue cooking as directed in Step 2.

2 tbsp	extra virgin olive oil	25 mL
12	large carrots, peeled and thinly sliced	12
12	cloves garlic, thinly sliced	12
½ tsp	salt	2 mL
½ tsp	freshly ground black pepper	2 mL
½ cup	drained capers	125 mL

1. In slow cooker stoneware, combine oil, carrots, garlic, salt and pepper. Toss to combine.

2. Cover and cook on **Low** for 6 hours or on **High** for 3 hours, until carrots are tender. Add capers and toss to combine. Serve immediately.

Variation

Braised Carrots with Black Olives
Substitute ½ cup (125 mL) chopped black olives, preferably kalamata, a particularly pungent Greek variety, for the capers.

Leeks à la Greque

Cooked this way, leeks are delicious hot or cold. They can be served as a vegetable or as part of an antipasto buffet.

• • • • •

Tip

To clean leeks, fill sink full of lukewarm water. Split leeks in half lengthwise and submerge in water, swishing them around to remove all traces of dirt. Transfer to a colander and rinse under cold water.

• • • • •

Make ahead

This dish can be made ahead and served chilled.

6	large leeks, white and light green part only, split lengthwise, cleaned and cut in half on the horizontal (see Tip, left)	6
¼ cup	olive oil	50 mL
2 tbsp	coriander seeds	25 mL
I tsp	cracked black peppercorns	5 mL
½ tsp	coarse sea salt	2 mL
¾ cup	dry white wine	175 mL
2	bay leaves	2

1. Place leeks in slow cooker stoneware.

2. In a saucepan, combine olive oil, coriander seeds, peppercorns, salt, white wine and bay leaves and bring to a boil. Pour mixture over leeks, cover and cook on **Low** for 6 to 8 hours or on **High** for 3 to 4 hours, until leeks are soft.

3. Using a slotted spoon, transfer leeks to a serving dish. Pour cooking liquid into a saucepan and, over high heat, bring to a boil. Boil rapidly for 5 minutes until sauce has reduced by half. Strain over leeks. Serve immediately or cover and chill thoroughly.

Peppery Red Onions

SERVES 4 TO 6

• • • • •

I love making this nippy treat in the autumn when the farmers' markets are brimming over with freshly harvested red onions. They are a tasty low-fat alternative to creamed onions. I particularly enjoy them as a topping for polenta or Grits 'n' Cheddar Cheese.

• • • • •

Tip

Use your favorite hot sauce, such as Tabasco, Louisiana Hot Sauce, Piri Piri, or try other more exotic brands to vary the flavors in this recipe.

4	large red onions, quartered	4
1 tbsp	extra virgin olive oil	15 mL
1 tsp	dried oregano leaves	5 mL
¼ cup	water or vegetable stock	50 mL
	Salt and black pepper, to taste	
	Hot pepper sauce, to taste (see Tip, left)	

1. In slow cooker stoneware, combine onions, olive oil, oregano, water or stock and salt and pepper. Stir thoroughly, cover and cook on **Low** for 8 hours or on **High** for 4 hours, until onions are tender.

2. Add hot sauce, toss well and serve.

Creamed Onions

Since long, slow cooking is the essence of getting the best out of onions, they have a natural affinity for the slow cooker. This simple, but elegant dish is a favorite with all members of my family. Whether you add cheese is simply a matter of taste. My family likes it equally well, with or without. Serve over polenta for a light main course.

Make ahead

This dish can be partially prepared the night before it is cooked. Complete Step 1 and refrigerate overnight. The next day, continue cooking as directed in Step 2.

2 tbsp	butter	25 mL
I tbsp	olive oil	15 mL
4 to 5	medium onions, quartered, about 2 lbs (1 kg)	4 to 5
2	sprigs fresh thyme or 1 tsp (5 mL) dried thyme leaves	2
½ tsp	salt	2 mL
½ tsp	freshly ground black pepper	2 mL
½ cup	vegetable stock	125 mL
½ cup	whipping (35%) cream	125 mL
¼ cup	freshly grated Parmesan cheese (optional)	50 mL
2 tbsp	finely chopped parsley	25 mL

1. In a large skillet, melt butter and oil over medium heat. Add onions and cook, stirring, until they begin to brown. Add thyme, salt and pepper and cook for 1 to 2 minutes. Add stock and bring to a boil.

2. Transfer contents of pan to slow cooker stoneware and cook on **Low** for 8 to 10 hours or on **High** for 4 to 5 hours, until onions are tender. Stir in cream and cheese, if using. Cover and cook on **High** for an additional 15 minutes. Garnish with parsley.

Creamy Mexican Beans

**SERVES 4 TO 6
AS A SIDE DISH**

• • • • • •

This rich side dish also does double duty as a main course. Serve it over rice or another grain, with a green salad for a delicious light meal. Because there are tomatoes in the sauce, which will toughen beans during cooking, dried lima beans should be cooked before being added to this recipe.

• • • • • •

Tip

If making this quantity, cook in a tall, narrow slow cooker to ensure that there is enough liquid to cover the beans. To serve as a main course, double the quantities and cook in a large slow cooker.

Be sure the cream cheese is very soft before you add it to the slow cooker. Otherwise, it will take too long to melt.

• • • • • •

Make ahead

This dish can be assembled the night before it is cooked but without adding the cream cheese. Complete Steps 1 and 2 and refrigerate overnight. The next day, continue cooking as directed in Step 3.

• Works best in a small (maximum 3½ quart) slow cooker (see Tip, left)

1 tbsp	vegetable oil	15 mL
2	onions, finely chopped	2
4	cloves garlic, minced	4
2	jalapeño peppers, finely chopped	2
1 tsp	dried oregano leaves	5 mL
1 tsp	cracked black peppercorns	5 mL
1 tsp	salt	5 mL
1	can (19 oz/540 mL) tomatoes, drained and coarsely chopped	1
1 tbsp	oil-packed sun-dried tomatoes, finely chopped	15 mL
1 cup	vegetable stock	250 mL
1 cup	frozen lima beans, thawed, or ½ cup (125 mL) dried lima beans, cooked and drained	250 mL
4 oz	cream cheese, softened and cut into 1-inch (2.5 cm) squares	125 g

1. In a skillet, heat oil over medium heat. Add onions and cook, stirring, until softened. Add garlic, jalapeño peppers, oregano, peppercorns and salt and cook, stirring, for 1 minute. Stir in tomatoes, sun-dried tomatoes and stock and bring to a boil.

2. Place beans in slow cooker stoneware and pour vegetable mixture over.

3. Cover and cook on **Low** for 8 hours or on **High** for 4 hours. Stir in cream cheese, cover and cook on **High** for 15 minutes, until cheese is melted and mixture is hot and bubbling.

Parsnip and Carrot Purée with Cumin

SERVES 8

• • • • •

The cumin adds a slightly exotic note to this traditional dish, which makes a great accompaniment to many foods.

• • • • •

Tip

In a dry skillet, toast cumin seeds until they release their aroma. Transfer to a spice grinder or mortar, or use the bottom of a measuring cup or wine bottle to coarsely grind.

• • • • •

Make ahead

Peel and cut parsnips and carrots. Cover and refrigerate overnight.

4 cups	peeled parsnips, cut into ½-inch (1 cm) cubes	1 L
2 cups	thinly sliced carrots	500 mL
1 tsp	cumin seeds, toasted and coarsely ground (see Tip, left)	5 mL
2 tbsp	butter or butter substitute	25 mL
1 tsp	granulated sugar	5 mL
½ tsp	salt	2 mL
¼ tsp	freshly ground black pepper	1 mL
¼ cup	water or vegetable stock	50 mL

1. In slow cooker stoneware, combine parsnips, carrots, cumin seeds, butter or butter substitute, sugar, salt, pepper and water or stock. Cover and cook on **Low** for 8 to 10 hours or on **High** for 4 to 5 hours, until vegetables are tender.

2. Using a potato masher or a food processor or blender, mash or purée mixture until smooth. Serve immediately.

Variation

Parsnip Purée with Cumin
Use 6 cups (1.5 L) cubed parsnips, instead of the parsnip-carrot combination.

Desserts

Rice Pudding with Cherries and Almonds

SERVES 6

• • • • •

This family favorite is delicious enough to serve at an elegant dinner party. Spoon into crystal goblets and serve warm or cold.

• • • • •

Tips

Long-grain white rice can be successfully used in this recipe, but the pudding will not be as creamy as one made with Arborio rice.

Use 1 cup (250 mL) fresh pitted cherries in place of the dried cherries, if desired. Or substitute an equal quantity of dried cranberries, instead.

For a richer pudding, use half milk and half cream.

• Lightly greased slow cooker stoneware

¾ cup	granulated sugar	175 mL
½ cup	Arborio rice (see Tips, left)	125 mL
¼ cup	dried cherries (see Tips, left)	50 mL
2 tbsp	ground almonds	25 mL
1 tsp	grated lemon zest	5 mL
Pinch	salt	Pinch
4 cups	milk (see Tips, left)	1 L
2	eggs	2
1 tsp	almond extract	5 mL
	Toasted sliced almonds (optional)	
	Whipped cream (optional)	

1. In prepared slow cooker stoneware, mix together sugar, rice, cherries, almonds, lemon zest and salt. Whisk together milk, eggs and almond extract, and stir into rice mixture. Cover and cook on **High** for 4 hours, until rice is tender and pudding is set. Serve warm, garnished with toasted almonds and whipped cream, if desired.

Maple Orange Pudding with Coconut

SERVES 4 TO 6

• • • • •

I love old-fashioned steamed puddings. For many years, these versatile treats fell into disfavor, likely due to their association with the ubiquitous suet puddings of Victorian times. In fact, good steamed puddings, which most resemble a warm, dense cake, are delectable comfort foods. Serve this hot with vanilla custard, frozen yogurt or ice cream and expect requests for seconds.

• • • • •

Tips

Orange peel, which is used in fruitcakes, is available in the baking section of the supermarket.

An English pudding basin is actually a simple rimmed bowl, most often white, that comes in various sizes. The rim is an asset as it enables you to make a seal with foil, which can be well secured with string or an elastic band.

• 6-cup (1.5 L) lightly greased pudding basin, mixing bowl or soufflé dish
• Large (minimum 5 quart) oval slow cooker

1½ cups	all-purpose flour	375 mL
1½ tsp	baking powder	7 mL
½ tsp	salt	2 mL
½ cup	butter, softened	125 mL
¾ cup	granulated sugar	175 mL
2	eggs	2
½ tsp	vanilla	2 mL
2 tbsp	chopped candied orange peel	25 mL
2 tbsp	milk	25 mL
½ cup	flaked coconut	125 mL
2 tbsp	orange marmalade	25 mL
2 tbsp	maple syrup	25 mL

1. In a bowl, mix together flour, baking powder and salt.

2. In another bowl, beat butter and sugar until smooth and creamy. Add eggs and beat until incorporated. Stir in vanilla and orange peel. Add flour mixture and beat until just blended. Stir in milk. Blend in coconut.

3. In a small saucepan over low heat, stir marmalade and maple syrup until marmalade dissolves and mixture is smooth. Place in bottom of prepared dish. Pour batter over top. Cover basin tightly with foil and secure with a string. Place basin in slow cooker stoneware and pour in enough boiling water to come 1 inch (2.5 cm) up the sides. Cover and cook on **High** for 3 to 4 hours, until a toothpick inserted in center of pudding comes out clean. Unmold and serve warm.

Bread Pudding in Caramel Sauce

SERVES 6

• • • • •

Nothing could be simpler than this delicious recipe for an old family favorite. Use leftover raisin bread for a more fulsome version. Serve hot or cold, depending on your preference.

• Lightly greased slow cooker stoneware

1 ½ cups	packed brown sugar	375 mL
¼ cup	butter, softened	50 mL
3	eggs	3
1 tsp	vanilla or 3 tbsp (45 mL) dark rum or whiskey	5 mL
1 tsp	ground cinnamon	5 mL
½ tsp	freshly grated nutmeg	2 mL
2 ½ cups	milk	625 mL
6	slices white bread, cut into 1-inch (2.5 cm) squares	6

1. In a bowl, beat sugar and butter until smooth and creamy. Add eggs, one at a time, and beat until incorporated. Add vanilla, cinnamon and nutmeg and beat until blended. Stir in milk.

2. In prepared slow cooker stoneware, place bread. Add milk mixture and stir to combine. Cover and cook on **High** for 4 hours.

Meredith's Molten Blondies *page 166* ➤

Raspberry Custard Cake

SERVES 6

• • • • •

This is a delicious old-fashioned dessert. As it cooks, the batter separates into a light soufflé-like layer on top, with a rich, creamy custard on the bottom. Serve hot or warm, accompanied by a light cookie, with whipped cream on the side, if desired.

• • • • •

Tip

I make this in a 7-inch (17.5 cm) square baking dish. The cooking times will vary in a differently proportioned dish.

- 6-cup (1.5 L) lightly greased baking or soufflé dish
- Large (minimum 5 quart) oval slow cooker

1 cup	granulated sugar, divided	250 mL
2 tbsp	butter, softened	25 mL
4	eggs, separated	4
	Grated zest and juice of 1 lemon	
Pinch	salt	Pinch
¼ cup	all-purpose flour	50 mL
1 cup	milk	250 mL
1½ cups	raspberries, thawed if frozen	375 mL
	Confectioner's (icing) sugar	

1. In a bowl, beat ¾ cup (175 mL) sugar with butter until light and fluffy. Beat in egg yolks until incorporated. Stir in lemon zest and juice. Add salt, then flour and mix until blended. Gradually add milk, beating to make a smooth batter.

2. In a separate bowl, with clean beaters, beat egg whites until soft peaks form. Add remaining ¼ cup (50 mL) sugar and beat until stiff peaks form. Fold into lemon mixture, then fold in raspberries.

3. Pour mixture into prepared dish. Cover with foil and tie tightly with a string. Place dish in slow cooker stoneware and add boiling water to come 1 inch (2.5 cm) up the sides. Cover and cook on **High** for 3 hours, until the cake springs back when touched lightly in the center. Dust lightly with confectioner's sugar and serve.

Variation

Blueberry Custard Cake
Substitute blueberries for the raspberries.

≺ Delectable Apple-Cranberry Coconut Crisp *page 172*

Sweet Potato Pecan Pie

SERVES 8

· · · · ·

I love everything about this mouth-watering dessert, which among its many charms, makes a great alternative to pumpkin pie. The gingersnap crust, the crunchy pecan topping and the creamy sweet potato filling are a delectable combination. Serve this hot or cold, with vanilla ice cream or whipped cream flavored with vanilla or brandy.

· · · · ·

Tip

If using a springform pan, ensure that water doesn't seep into the cake by wrapping the bottom of the pan in one large seamless piece of foil that extends up the sides and over the top. Cover the top with a single piece of foil that extends down the sides and secure with string.

- 7-inch (17.5 cm) well-greased springform pan (see Tip, left) or 7-inch (17.5 cm) 6-cup (1.5 L) soufflé dish, lined with greased heavy-duty foil
- Heavy-duty foil, if using a springform pan
- Large (minimum 5 quart) oval slow cooker

CRUST

1 cup	gingersnap cookie crumbs	250 mL
3 tbsp	packed brown sugar	45 mL
1/2 tsp	ground ginger	2 mL
3 tbsp	melted butter	45 mL

FILLING

2	medium sweet potatoes, cooked, peeled and puréed (about 2 cups/500 mL)	2
1/2 cup	packed brown sugar	125 mL
2	eggs, beaten	2
1/2 tsp	ground cinnamon	2 mL
1/4 tsp	ground allspice	1 mL
Pinch	salt	Pinch

TOPPING

1/2 cup	chopped pecans	125 mL
1/4 cup	packed brown sugar	50 mL
2 tbsp	melted butter	25 mL

1. **Crust:** In a bowl, combine gingersnap crumbs, brown sugar and ginger. Add butter and mix well. Press mixture into the bottom of prepared pan. Place in freezer until ready for use.

2. **Filling:** In a bowl, beat sweet potatoes, brown sugar, eggs, cinnamon, allspice and salt until smooth. Spread evenly over prepared crust.

3. Topping: In a bowl, combine pecans and brown sugar. Drizzle with butter and stir until combined. Sprinkle over top of pie. Place a layer of parchment or waxed paper over top of cake and cover tightly with foil.

4. Place pan in slow cooker stoneware and pour in enough boiling water to come 1 inch (2.5 cm) up the sides. Cover and cook on **High** for 4 hours, until filling is set. Serve warm or cold.

Cranberry Apricot Upside-Down Cake

SERVES 6

• • • • •

Keep cranberries in the freezer and dried apricots in the cupboard and you can make this delicious cake year-round from pantry ingredients. Serve with whipped cream or vanilla ice cream.

• • • • •

Tip

To prevent accumulated moisture from dripping on the cake batter, place two clean tea towels, each folded in half (so you will have four layers), across the top of the slow cooker stoneware before covering. The towels will absorb the moisture generated during cooking.

1/4 cup	melted butter	50 mL
1/2 cup	packed brown sugar	125 mL
1/4 cup	finely chopped walnuts or pecans	50 mL
1 1/2 cups	cranberries, thawed if frozen	375 mL
3/4 cup	chopped dried apricots	175 mL

CAKE

1 1/4 cups	all-purpose flour	300 mL
2 tsp	baking powder	10 mL
1/4 tsp	salt	1 mL
1/4 cup	butter, softened	50 mL
3/4 cup	granulated sugar	175 mL
1	egg	1
1 tsp	vanilla	5 mL
1/2 cup	milk	125 mL

1. In a small bowl, combine butter, brown sugar and walnuts. Spread over bottom of prepared slow cooker stoneware. Arrange cranberries and apricots on top.

2. Cake: In a bowl, mix together flour, baking powder and salt. In a mixing bowl, using an electric mixer if desired, cream butter and sugar until light and fluffy. Beat in egg and vanilla until incorporated. Add flour mixture alternately with milk, beating well after each addition. Pour mixture over fruit.

3. Place tea towels over top of stoneware (see Tip, left). Cover and cook on **High** for 2 1/2 hours or until a toothpick inserted in center of cake comes out clean.

4. When ready to serve, slice and invert on plate. Top with vanilla ice cream.

Blueberry Semolina Cake with Maple Syrup

SERVES 6

• • • • •

This delicious cake, which is great for snacking as well as dessert, owes its origins to Greek cuisine. In Greece, cakes made from semolina, the durum wheat from which pasta is made, are traditionally soaked in flavored sugar syrup. This version simplifies the process by using maple syrup instead. Serve warm or at room temperature.

• • • • •

Tips

One challenge with making cakes in a slow cooker is finding a baking pan that will fit. I have made this recipe in both a 7-inch (17.5 cm) square baking dish and an 8½-by 4½-inch (21 by 11 cm) loaf pan with good results.

For best results, put a layer of parchment paper in the bottom of the baking pan before adding the batter, to facilitate easy removal.

Semolina is available at natural foods stores or supermarkets with a good selection of grains.

• Greased baking dish or loaf pan (see Tips, left)
• Large (minimum 5 quart) oval slow cooker

I cup	durum semolina (see Tips, left)	250 mL
I tsp	baking powder	5 mL
¾ cup	granulated sugar	175 mL
⅓ cup	butter, softened	75 mL
2	eggs, separated	2
I tsp	vanilla	5 mL
¾ cup	plain yogurt	175 mL
I cup	blueberries	250 mL
Pinch	salt	Pinch
½ cup	maple syrup	125 mL

1. In a bowl, mix together semolina and baking powder.

2. In a separate bowl, beat sugar and butter until smooth and creamy. Beat in egg yolks until incorporated. Stir in vanilla. Add semolina mixture alternately with yogurt, mixing well after each addition. Fold in blueberries. In another bowl, with clean beaters, beat egg whites with salt until stiff peaks form, then fold into batter. Spread mixture evenly in prepared dish and cover tightly with foil, securing with a string.

3. Place in slow cooker stoneware and pour in enough boiling water to come 1 inch (2.5 cm) up the sides. Cover and cook on **High** for 3 to 4 hours or until a toothpick inserted in center of cake comes out clean.

4. Turn out onto a serving plate and pour maple syrup evenly over top. Serve warm or allow to cool.

Meredith's Molten Blondies

SERVES 6 TO 8

• • • • •

A blondie is a brownie flavored with butterscotch instead of chocolate. This variation transforms that idea into a delectable dessert with cake on the top and sauce on the bottom. It is superb over vanilla ice cream. I have my daughter, Meredith, to thank for the idea of enhancing the recipe with chocolate chips, which are a great addition. Butterscotch chips or a combination of butterscotch and chocolate is equally delicious. This can also be served cold, with whipped cream.

I cup	all-purpose flour	250 mL
I tsp	baking powder	5 mL
½ tsp	salt	2 mL
2 cups	packed brown sugar, divided	500 mL
¼ cup	butter	50 mL
I tsp	vanilla	5 mL
½ cup	milk	125 mL
½ cup	chocolate or butterscotch chips	125 mL
½ cup	chopped walnuts or pecans (optional)	125 mL
I cup	boiling water	250 mL

1. In a bowl, mix together flour, baking powder and salt.

2. In a separate bowl, beat 1 cup (250 mL) brown sugar with butter until creamy. Stir in vanilla. Add dry ingredients alternately with milk, beating well after each addition. Stir in chips and walnuts, if using. Spread mixture evenly in prepared slow cooker stoneware.

3. In a heatproof measure, combine remaining brown sugar and boiling water. Pour over batter. Cover and cook on **High** for 2½ to 3 hours, until cake layer looks cooked. Serve warm with vanilla ice cream.

Italian-Style Cornmeal Cake with Orange

SERVES 6 TO 8

● ● ● ● ● ●

This is a delicious light cake. It makes a perfect finish to a great meal and is excellent to have on hand for snacking.

● ● ● ● ●

Tip

Although the orange glaze is a nice finish to this cake, it is also very tasty without a glaze. Allow cake to cool, unmold and dust lightly with confectioner's sugar.

- 7-inch (17.5 cm) well-greased springform pan or 7-inch (17.5 cm) 6-cup (1.5 L) soufflé or baking dish, lined with greased heavy-duty foil
- Large (minimum 5 quart) oval slow cooker

1 cup	fine cornmeal	250 mL
1/4 cup	finely chopped walnuts or pecans	50 mL
2 tsp	baking powder	10 mL
1/2 tsp	salt	2 mL
3/4 cup	granulated sugar	175 mL
1/2 cup	butter, softened	125 mL
2	eggs	2
1 tsp	vanilla	5 mL
1 tbsp	grated orange zest	15 mL
1/4 cup	plain yogurt	50 mL

ORANGE GLAZE (OPTIONAL)

1/2 cup	confectioner's (icing) sugar, sifted	125 mL
1/4 cup	orange juice	50 mL
1 tbsp	orange-flavored liqueur (optional)	15 mL

1. In a bowl, mix together cornmeal, walnuts, baking powder and salt.

2. In another bowl, beat sugar and butter until light and fluffy. Beat in eggs until incorporated. Stir in vanilla and orange zest. Add dry ingredients in two additions alternately with yogurt, mixing until blended. Spoon batter into prepared pan. Wrap securely in foil (see Tips, page 162) and cook on **High** for 4 hours, until cake is puffed and pulling away from side of pan. Glaze cake, if desired.

3. Orange Glaze: In a bowl, combine confectioner's sugar, orange juice and orange-flavored liqueur, if using. With a skewer, poke several holes in the cake. Spread glaze over hot cake.

4. Let cake cool in pan for 30 minutes, then unmold.

Spiced Pears Baked in Red Wine

SERVES 6 TO 8

• • • • •

This classic light dessert, which makes an elegant finish to any meal, fills your house with a wonderful aroma as it cooks. It's a snap to make and festive enough for any celebration. Although it's tasty enough to serve solely with vanilla wafers, for special occasions, I like to serve a cheese course as an accompaniment.

• • • • •

Tip

Rub pears with lemon juice after they are peeled to prevent discoloring or place a piece of parchment directly on top of pears to ensure more even color.

• • • • •

Make ahead

This should be made early in the day or the night before so it can be well chilled before serving.

• Works best in a 3½-quart slow cooker, which ensures that the pears will be appropriately submerged in the wine

6 to 8	pears, peeled, cored and cut in half lengthwise	6 to 8
2 cups	dry red wine, or more, if necessary, to cover pears	500 mL
½ cup	granulated sugar	125 mL
1	cinnamon stick piece, about 2 inches (5 cm)	1
4	whole cloves	4
	Zest of 1 orange	

1. Place pears in slow cooker stoneware. Add wine (enough to cover pears), sugar, cinnamon, cloves and orange zest. Cover and cook on **Low** for 6 to 8 hours, until pears are tender. Chill well and serve.

Chocolate Flan with Toasted Almonds

SERVES 6

• • • • •

Here's a deliciously decadent chocolate dessert. Save it for special occasions or treat yourself and enjoy.

• 6-cup (1.5 L) lightly greased mold or soufflé dish
• Large (minimum 5 quart) oval slow cooker

CARAMEL

½ cup	granulated sugar	125 mL
2 tbsp	water	25 mL
1 tbsp	freshly squeezed lemon juice	15 mL
¼ cup	toasted slivered almonds	50 mL

FLAN

3½ oz	bittersweet chocolate, broken into chunks	105 g
1 cup	whipping cream	250 mL
1 cup	milk	250 mL
⅓ cup	granulated sugar	75 mL
2	eggs	2
2	egg yolks	2

1. Caramel: In a heavy-bottomed saucepan over medium heat, cook sugar and water until mixture becomes a deep shade of nutmeg. Standing well back from dish, add lemon juice and stir until bubbles subside. Pour into prepared dish and, working quickly, tip mixture around the dish until sides are well coated. Sprinkle almonds over bottom of dish and set aside.

2. Flan: In a heatproof bowl, place chocolate. In a clean saucepan, bring cream, milk and sugar to a boil. Pour over chocolate and stir until mixture is smooth and chocolate is melted.

3. In a bowl, beat eggs and egg yolks. Gradually add chocolate mixture, beating constantly until incorporated. Strain mixture into caramel-coated dish. Cover with foil and secure with string. Place dish in slow cooker stoneware and add enough boiling water to come 1 inch (2.5 cm) up the sides. Cover and cook on **High** for 2 to 2½ hours, or until a knife inserted in custard comes out clean. Remove and refrigerate for 4 hours or overnight.

4. When ready to serve, remove foil. Run a sharp knife around the edge of the flan and invert onto a serving plate. Serve with whipped cream, if desired.

Apricot Almond Pudding

SERVES 6

· · · · ·

This variation on an old English pudding is rich and satisfying without being heavy. Serve with vanilla custard, frozen yogurt or ice cream for an unusual and delicious dessert.

- 6-cup (1.5 L) lightly greased pudding basin, mixing bowl or soufflé dish
- Large (minimum 5 quart) oval slow cooker

1 ½ cups	all-purpose flour	375 mL
¼ cup	ground almonds	50 mL
1 ½ tsp	baking powder	7 mL
½ tsp	salt	2 mL
1 tsp	ground ginger	5 mL
½ cup	butter, softened	125 mL
¾ cup	granulated sugar	175 mL
2	eggs	2
1 tsp	almond extract	5 mL
2 tbsp	milk	25 mL
¼ cup	dried cherries, cranberries or raisins	50 mL
2 tbsp	apricot jam	25 mL
1 tbsp	amaretto liqueur or liquid honey	15 mL
	Vanilla ice cream or custard	

1. In a bowl, mix together flour, almonds, baking powder, salt and ginger.

2. In another bowl, beat butter and sugar until smooth and creamy. Add eggs and beat until incorporated. Stir in almond extract. Add flour mixture in two additions alternately with milk, beating just until blended. Stir in cherries.

3. In a small saucepan over low heat, stir apricot jam and amaretto until jam is dissolved and mixture is smooth. Pour into the bottom of prepared dish. Spoon batter over top. Cover basin tightly with foil and secure with a string. Place dish in slow cooker stoneware and pour in enough boiling water to come 1 inch (2.5 cm) up the sides. Cover and cook on **High** for 3 to 4 hours, until a toothpick inserted in center of pudding comes out clean.

4. When ready to serve, run a knife around the edge of the pudding and unmold. Slice and serve with vanilla ice cream or custard.

Cranberry-Red Currant Crumb Pudding

SERVES 6

• • • • •

Don't discard that slightly stale bread. Here is another great recipe for transforming leftover bread into a delicious dessert.

• 6-cup (1.5 L) lightly greased pudding basin, baking or soufflé dish
• Large (minimum 5 quart) oval slow cooker

2 cups	milk	500 mL
¾ cup	granulated sugar	175 mL
2 tbsp	butter	25 mL
2 cups	fresh bread crumbs	500 mL
3	eggs	3
1 tsp	vanilla	5 mL
¼ tsp	salt	1 mL
¼ cup	dried cranberries or raisins	50 mL
2 tbsp	red currant jelly, stirred until smooth	25 mL

1. In a saucepan over medium heat, bring milk, sugar and butter to a boil, stirring, until butter melts. Remove from heat. Stir in bread crumbs.

2. In a bowl, beat eggs, vanilla and salt. Stir in cranberries, then ¼ cup (50 mL) bread crumb mixture. Add remaining bread crumb mixture and stir to blend.

3. Place red currant jelly in bottom of prepared dish. Add bread crumb mixture. Cover with foil and tie tightly with string. Place dish in slow cooker stoneware and add boiling water to come 1 inch (2.5 cm) up the sides. Cover and cook on **High** for 2½ hours, until toothpick inserted in center of pudding comes out clean.

Delectable Apple-Cranberry Coconut Crisp

SERVES 6 TO 8

• • • • •

I love to make this delicious dessert in the fall when apples and cranberries are in season. This version is a little tart, which suits my taste, but if you have a sweet tooth, add more sugar to the cranberry mixture. Great on its own, this is even better with whipped cream or a scoop of frozen yogurt or vanilla ice cream.

• Lightly greased slow cooker stoneware

4 cups	sliced, peeled apples	1 L
2 cups	cranberries, thawed if frozen	500 mL
½ cup	granulated sugar	125 mL
1 tbsp	cornstarch	15 mL
½ tsp	ground cinnamon	2 mL
2 tbsp	freshly squeezed lemon juice or port wine	25 mL

COCONUT TOPPING

½ cup	packed brown sugar	125 mL
½ cup	rolled oats	125 mL
¼ cup	flaked sweetened coconut	50 mL
¼ cup	butter	50 mL

1. In a bowl, combine apples, cranberries, sugar, cornstarch, cinnamon and lemon juice or port. Mix well and transfer to prepared stoneware.

2. Coconut Topping: In a separate bowl, combine brown sugar, rolled oats, coconut and butter. Using two forks or your fingers, combine until crumbly. Spread over apple mixture.

3. Place two clean tea towels, each folded in half (so you will have four layers) over top of stoneware. Cover and cook on **High** for 3 to 4 hours, until crisp is hot and bubbling. Serve with whipped cream or ice cream, if desired.

Variation
Apple-Coconut Crisp
Use 6 cups (1.5 L) of sliced apples, reduce sugar to ¼ cup (50 mL) and use lemon juice rather than port wine.

Blueberry-Rhubarb Spoonbread

SERVES 6 TO 8

• • • • •

I love this delicious variation on old-fashioned spoonbread. Serve over vanilla ice cream or with sweetened whipped cream and expect requests for seconds.

• • • • •

Tip

To prevent accumulated moisture from dripping on the cake batter, place two clean tea towels, each folded in half (so you will have four layers), across the top of the slow cooker stoneware before covering. The towels will absorb the moisture generated during cooking.

• Lightly greased slow cooker stoneware
• Large (minimum 5 quart) oval slow cooker

2 cups	blueberries, thawed if frozen	500 mL
2 cups	rhubarb, cut into 1-inch (2.5 cm) chunks, thawed if frozen	500 mL
1/4 cup	granulated sugar	50 mL
1 tsp	ground cinnamon	5 mL
	Zest and juice of 1 orange	

CORNBREAD

1 cup	cornmeal	250 mL
1 1/2 tsp	baking powder	7 mL
Pinch	salt	Pinch
1/2 cup	softened butter	125 mL
1/2 cup	granulated sugar	125 mL
2	eggs	2
1 tsp	vanilla	5 mL

1. In a bowl, combine blueberries, rhubarb, sugar, cinnamon, orange zest and juice. Set aside.

2. Cornbread: In a separate bowl, combine cornmeal, baking powder and salt. In a mixing bowl, beat together butter and sugar until light and fluffy. Add cornmeal mixture. Add eggs, one at a time, and mix until well blended. Stir in vanilla.

3. Spread batter over bottom of stoneware. Spoon berries over top. Place tea towels over top of stoneware (see Tip, left). Cover and cook on **High** for 3 hours, until batter is browning around the edges and spoonbread is set.

Variation

Blueberry Spoonbread

Use 4 cups (1 L) blueberries and reduce sugar to 2 tbsp (25 mL). Substitute 2 tbsp (25 mL) lemon juice and 1 tbsp (15 mL) lemon zest for the orange.

Rhubarb Betty

SERVES 6

There are many different variations on this traditional dessert, which is basically baked fruit with a seasoned topping. This version, which relies on bread crumbs for its starch component, is particularly simple and good. It works equally well with a rhubarb-strawberry combination or with apples. Serve with sweetened whipped cream.

Tips

If you have a large oval cooker, double the quantity. Refrigerate leftovers and reheat.

Fresh bread crumbs are far superior to the ready-made kind, which can be very dry. They are easily made in a food processor by removing the crust, if desired, cutting the bread into manageable chunks and then processing until the appropriate degree of fineness is achieved. Tightly covered, bread crumbs will keep for two or three days in the refrigerator.

- Lightly greased slow cooker stoneware
- Works best in a 3½-quart slow cooker (see Tips, right)

⅓ cup	melted butter	75 mL
2 cups	fresh bread crumbs (see Tips, right)	500 mL
4 cups	rhubarb, cut into 1-inch (2.5 cm) chunks	1 L
1 cup	granulated sugar	250 mL
1 tbsp	all-purpose flour	15 mL
1 tsp	ground cinnamon	5 mL
	Zest and juice of 1 orange	

1. In a mixing bowl, combine butter and bread crumbs. Set aside.

2. In a separate bowl, combine rhubarb, sugar, flour and cinnamon.

3. In prepared slow cooker stoneware, layer one-third of bread-crumb mixture, then one-half of rhubarb mixture. Repeat layers of bread crumbs and fruit, then finish with a layer of bread crumbs on top. Pour zest and orange juice over top. Cook on **High** for 3 to 4 hours, until bubbling and brown.

Variations

Rhubarb-Strawberry Betty
Use 2 cups (500 mL) each of strawberries, quartered, and rhubarb, cut into 1-inch (2.5 cm) lengths. Reduce sugar to ¾ cup (175 mL) and omit cinnamon.

Apple Betty
Substitute apple slices for rhubarb and the juice and zest of one lemon for the orange. Reduce sugar to ½ to ¾ cup (125 to 175 mL), depending on preference.

Bread Pudding with Raspberry Sauce

SERVES 6 TO 8

• • • • • •

This easy-to-make version of bread pudding takes a comfort-food classic and, with the simple addition of a rich raspberry sauce, makes it into a much more sophisticated dessert. While it may not be like the one your grandmother used to make, expect your guests to request seconds.

• Lightly greased slow cooker stoneware

6 cups	stale bread, cut into 1-inch (2.5 cm) cubes	1.5 L
3 tbsp	melted butter	45 mL
4	eggs	4
¾ cup	granulated sugar	175 mL
4 cups	milk	1 L
½ tsp	ground cinnamon	2 mL
½ tsp	vanilla	2 mL

RASPBERRY SAUCE

¼ cup	granulated sugar	50 mL
¼ cup	water	50 mL
2 cups	raspberries, thawed if frozen	500 mL
1 tsp	balsamic vinegar	5 mL

1. In prepared stoneware, combine bread and melted butter. Toss to mix thoroughly.

2. In a large bowl, beat eggs. Mix in sugar, milk, cinnamon and vanilla. Pour over bread cubes. Cover and cook on **High** for 4 hours, until top is golden brown.

3. Raspberry Sauce: In a saucepan, combine sugar and water. Bring to a boil. Cook for 1 minute or until sugar is thoroughly dissolved and mixture is becoming syrupy. Add raspberries. Return to a boil and cook until raspberries fall apart when crushed with a wooden spoon. (This will take several minutes, depending upon the size of the pot.) Remove from heat and stir in balsamic vinegar. If you prefer a smooth sauce, purée in a food processor.

4. Spoon pudding into individual bowls and top with sauce.

Lemony Banana Custard

SERVES 4 TO 6

• • • • •

Just wait until you try this luscious combination of bananas and lemon in a creamy custard base. It's my idea of comfort food. Even better, it's so easy to make, you can enjoy it every day of the week.

• Lightly greased slow cooker stoneware

¾ cup	granulated sugar	175 mL
2 tbsp	freshly squeezed lemon juice	25 mL
¼ cup	water	50 mL
⅓ cup	butter	75 mL
2	eggs	2
½ tsp	ground cinnamon	2 mL
8	bananas, mashed	8
	Finely chopped pecans or walnuts (optional)	
	Sweetened whipped cream (optional)	

1. In a saucepan, over medium heat, bring sugar, lemon juice and water to a boil. Cook, stirring until a light syrup forms, about 5 minutes. Set aside.

2. In a mixing bowl, using an electric mixer, if desired, cream together butter and eggs. Gradually fold into warm syrup. Add cinnamon and bananas and stir to combine. Pour mixture into prepared stoneware. Cover and cook on **High** for 3 hours, until mixture sets. When ready to serve, garnish with chopped pecans or walnuts, if using, and top with a dollop of sweetened whipped cream.

Maple Surprise

SERVES 6

• • • • •

Served over vanilla ice cream, this delicious sauce makes a great way to finish a meal. If you don't identify the key ingredient for your guests, they'll enjoy guessing. Most will think it's a particularly good applesauce, but won't be able to pinpoint the unusual flavoring. You can also serve this on its own with a good dollop of whipped cream.

• • • • •

Tip

Candied ginger is usually available in the bulk food section of supermarkets.

4 cups	squash or pumpkin, peeled and cut into 1-inch (2.5 cm) cubes	1 L
1/4 cup	melted butter	50 mL
Pinch	salt	Pinch
1 tbsp	dark or amber rum or 1/2 tsp (2 mL) vanilla	15 mL
1 cup	maple syrup	250 mL
	Vanilla ice cream (optional)	
3 tbsp	walnuts, finely chopped	45 mL
3 tbsp	candied ginger, finely chopped (see Tip, right)	45 mL

1. In slow cooker stoneware, combine squash or pumpkin, butter, salt, rum or vanilla and maple syrup. Cover and cook on **Low** for 8 hours or on **High** for 4 hours, until squash is very tender.

2. With a wooden spoon or potato masher, crush mixture to a smooth purée. Spoon over vanilla ice cream, if desired, and top with walnuts and ginger.

Ginger Sponge Pudding

• • • • •

This light and delicious sponge-like pudding cake is wonderful on its own, topped with a dollop of whipped cream or as an accompaniment for fresh berries. It's easy to make, and so long as you have candied ginger on hand, it can be assembled with pantry ingredients.

• • • • •

Tips

"Chop" the ginger in a food processor. Combine with milk and process until the desired fineness is achieved.

Candied ginger is usually available in the bulk food section of supermarkets.

I make this in a 7-inch (17.5 cm) square baking dish. The cooking times will vary in a differently proportioned dish.

• 6-cup (1.5 L) lightly greased pudding mold, baking or soufflé dish
• Large (minimum 5 quart) oval slow cooker

¼ cup	butter	50 mL
¼ cup	granulated sugar	50 mL
3	eggs, separated	3
½ tsp	vanilla	2 mL
½ cup	all-purpose flour	125 mL
I tsp	baking powder	5 mL
½ tsp	ground ginger	2 mL
Pinch	salt	Pinch
I cup	milk	250 mL
¾ cup	candied ginger, finely chopped	175 mL

1. In a mixing bowl, using an electric mixer, if desired, cream butter and sugar, until fluffy. Add egg yolks one at a time and beat until smooth. Add vanilla and stir to combine thoroughly.

2. In a separate bowl, combine flour, baking powder, ground ginger and salt. Add to butter mixture alternately with milk, mixing well after each addition. Stir in chopped ginger. Alternately, add candied ginger with milk, if chopped in food processor (see Tip, left).

3. In a separate bowl, beat egg whites until stiff. Gently fold into flour mixture to make a smooth batter. Spoon into prepared dish. Cover with lid or foil and secure with string or an elastic band.

4. Place in dish in slow cooker stoneware and pour in enough boiling water to come 1 inch (2.5 cm) up the sides of bowl. Cover and cook on **High** for 2½ to 3 hours or until a toothpick inserted in center of cake comes out clean. Turn out on a plate and serve with sweetened whipped cream or fresh berries.

Just Peachy Gingerbread Upside-Down Cake

SERVES 10 TO 12

• • • • •

The deliciously rich molasses-flavored gingerbread, topped with peaches in caramel, is an absolutely irresistible combination. Serve it with a big scoop of vanilla ice cream and savor every bite.

• • • • •

Tips

To prevent accumulated moisture from dripping on the cake batter, place two clean tea towels, each folded in half (so you will have four layers), across the top of the slow cooker stoneware before covering. The towels will absorb the moisture generated during cooking.

Use 4 cups (1 L) sliced peeled peaches if you prefer.

• Lightly greased slow cooker stoneware

¼ cup	melted butter	50 mL
½ cup	packed brown sugar	125 mL
2	cans (each 14 oz/398 mL) sliced peaches, drained (see Tips, left)	2

CAKE

2 cups	all-purpose flour	500 mL
2 tsp	baking soda	10 mL
½ tsp	salt	2 mL
1 tbsp	ground ginger	15 mL
1 tsp	ground cinnamon	5 mL
½ cup	molasses	125 mL
½ cup	boiling water	125 mL
½ cup	butter, softened	125 mL
1 cup	packed brown sugar	250 mL
1	egg	1

1. In a bowl, combine butter and brown sugar. Spread over bottom of prepared stoneware. Arrange peaches on top.

2. Cake: In a bowl, combine flour, baking soda, salt, ginger and cinnamon. In a separate bowl, combine molasses and boiling water. In a mixing bowl, beat butter and brown sugar until smooth and creamy. Beat in egg until incorporated. Add flour mixture alternately with molasses mixture, beating well after each addition. Pour batter over peaches.

3. Place tea towels over top of the slow cooker stoneware (see Tips, left). Cover and cook on **High** for 3 hours or until a toothpick inserted in center of cake comes out clean. When ready to serve, slice and invert onto plate. Top with vanilla ice cream.

Variation
Apple Gingerbread Upside-Down Cake
Substitute 4 cups (1 L) chopped peeled apples for the peaches.

National Library of Canada Cataloguing in Publication

Finlayson, Judith
    125 best vegetarian slow cooker recipes / Judith Finlayson.

Includes index.
ISBN 0-7788-0104-7

1. Vegetarian cookery. 2. Electric cookery, Slow.
I. Title. II. Title: One hundred twenty-five best vegetarian slow cooker recipes.

TX837.F55 2004   641.5'636   C2004-902434-5

Index

More Great Books from Robert Rose

Appliance Cooking

- 125 Best Microwave Oven Recipes
  by Johanna Burkhard
- 125 Best Pressure Cooker Recipes
  by Cinda Chavich
- The 150 Best Slow Cooker Recipes
  by Judith Finlayson
- Delicious & Dependable Slow Cooker Recipes
  by Judith Finlayson
- 125 Best Vegetarian Slow Cooker Recipes
  by Judith Finlayson
- America's Best Slow Cooker Recipes
  by Donna-Marie Pye
- Canada's Best Slow Cooker Recipes
  by Donna-Marie Pye
- The Best Family Slow Cooker Recipes
  by Donna-Marie Pye
- 125 Best Indoor Grill Recipes
  by Ilana Simon
- The Best Convection Oven Cookbook
  by Linda Stephen
- 125 Best Toaster Oven Recipes
  by Linda Stephen
- 250 Best American Bread Machine Baking Recipes
  by Donna Washburn and Heather Butt
- 250 Best Canadian Bread Machine Baking Recipes
  by Donna Washburn and Heather Butt

Baking

- 250 Best Cakes & Pies
  by Esther Brody
- 250 Best Cobblers, Custards, Cupcakes, Bread Puddings & More
  by Esther Brody
- 500 Best Cookies, Bars & Squares
  by Esther Brody
- 500 Best Muffin Recipes
  by Esther Brody
- 125 Best Cheesecake Recipes
  by George Geary
- 125 Best Chocolate Recipes
  by Julie Hasson
- 125 Best Chocolate Chip Recipes
  by Julie Hasson
- Cake Mix Magic
  by Jill Snider
- Cake Mix Magic 2
  by Jill Snider

Healthy Cooking

- 125 Best Vegetarian Recipes
  by Byron Ayanoglu with contributions from Alexis Kemezys
- The Juicing Bible
  by Pat Crocker and Susan Eagles
- The Smoothies Bible
  by Pat Crocker
- Better Baby Food
  by Daina Kalnins, RD, CNSD and Joanne Saab, RD
- Better Food for Kids
  by Daina Kalnins, RD, CNSD and Joanne Saab, RD

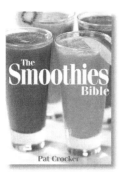

- 500 Best Healthy Recipes
  Edited by Lynn Roblin, RD
- 125 Best Gluten-Free Recipes
  by Donna Washburn and Heather Butt
- America's Everyday Diabetes Cookbook
  Edited by Katherine E. Younker, MBA, RD
- Canada's Everyday Diabetes Choice Recipes
  Edited by Katherine E. Younker, MBA, RD
- The Diabetes Choice Cookbook for Canadians
  Edited by Katherine E. Younker, MBA, RD
- The Best Diabetes Cookbook (U.S.)
  Edited by Katherine E. Younker, MBA, RD

Recent Bestsellers

- 300 Best Comfort Food Recipes
  by Johanna Burkhard
- The Convenience Cook
  by Judith Finlayson
- The Spice and Herb Bible
  by Ian Hemphill
- 125 Best Ice Cream Recipes
  by Marilyn Linton and Tanya Linton
- 125 Best Casseroles & One-Pot Meals
  by Rose Murray
- The Cook's Essential Kitchen Dictionary
  by Jacques Rolland

- 125 Best Ground Meat Recipes
  by Ilana Simon
- Easy Indian Cooking
  by Suneeta Vaswani
- Simply Thai Cooking
  by Wandee Young and Byron Ayanoglu

Health

- The Complete Natural Medicine Guide to the 50 Most Common Medicinal Herbs
  by Dr. Heather Boon, B.Sc.Phm., Ph.D. and Michael Smith, B.Pharm, M.R.Pharm.S., ND
- The Complete Kid's Allergy and Asthma Guide
  Edited by Dr. Milton Gold
- The Complete Natural Medicine Guide to Breast Cancer
  by Sat Dharam Kaur, ND
- The Complete Doctor's Stress Solution
  by Penny Kendall-Reed, MSc, ND and Dr. Stephen Reed, MD, FRCSC
- The Complete Doctor's Healthy Back Bible
  by Dr. Stephen Reed, MD and Penny Kendall-Reed, MSc, ND with Dr. Michael Ford, MD, FRCSC and Dr. Charles Gregory, MD, ChB, FRCP(C)
- Everyday Risks in Pregnancy & Breastfeeding
  by Dr. Gideon Koren, MD, FRCP(C), ND

Also Available
from Robert Rose

The **convenience cook**

125 Best Recipes
for Easy Homemade Meals Using Time-Saving
Foods from Boxes, Bottles, Cans & More

Judith Finlayson

For more great books see previous pages